HOW TO
HOOK UP WITH
AND DATE BEAUTIFUL
WOMEN

BY DENNIS PARK

ISBN: 978-1-946402-02-8

Interior design by booknook.biz

To The Most High. Thank you for a second chance.

To the Golden State of California. Thank you for the energy, the inspiration, the weather, and the weed.

To the game. Thank you for levelling the sexual playing field despite the obstacles others have set before me.

To Walter and Lillian. Thank you for loving me during my dusty days.

To the Metro bus, light rail, and subway operators. Thank you for keeping the city moving.

"Only a fool trips on what is behind him." — Iceberg Slim

Contents

CHAPTER 1
A Word To The Reader

Greetings and salutations. My name is Dennis Park, your guide and host on this journey, and it's good to meet you. Life is the sweetest madness you will ever know, and I trust all is well with you. I send love and goodwill from Los Angeles, California, and I want to thank everyone reading these words right now.

Perhaps you purchased this book from Amazon. Perhaps you purchased this book from a brick and mortar bookstore. Perhaps you received it as a gift or borrowed it from a friend with no real intention of returning it because you struggle to enjoy sexual success with women. Whatever the case may be, thank you for taking some of the priceless time out of your life to spend with this book and the game contained within.

Why did I write *How To Hook Up With And Date Beautiful Women*? More than a few of my friends, family members, and fellow writers asked me that question because they couldn't understand why I felt compelled to write this book. Here are the four criticisms I heard repeatedly:

- Writing a dating book is a waste of time. There's way too many of those books on the market already.
- Fathers should teach their sons how to date.
- The game is bullshit. Why are you trying to turn men into pimps, players, and womanisers?
- What makes you an expert to write on this, Dennis?

Let's knock these feather-headed quibbles down one by one, shall we?

First, writing a book about dating is not a waste of time. Especially if it's a well-written work which addresses the experiences of its readers in a way they can relate to personally. Especially if it's a well-written work which provides solutions to the problems they struggle with.

Dating is much more than taking someone out to dinner and a movie and trying to get lucky. Dating is a ritual of romance. Dating requires confidence and social skills you can develop and master through study and hands-on experience if you care enough to make the effort.

There are plenty of men who aren't interested in making that effort. At all. There are plenty of men who aren't interested in dating. At all. These are men in monogamous relationships who don't cheat. Men who went MGTOW. Happily married men. Millions of men who believe they already know everything they need to know about dating.

That's fine. What those men feel and think has absolutely nothing to do with you and the beautiful girl you didn't fuck this past weekend because you were too afraid to approach her for casual sex. This is about you. The game is about you.

If dating wasn't so important to men across America, how are some dating coaches earning $20,000-$30,000 a month? Or more? The lust which drives men to pursue and have sex with women provides dating coaches with multiple streams of income which include book sales (audiobook, eBook, and paperback), consultation fees, and speaking engagements.

Skilled writers craft books which clearly convey their ideas and passions to readers around the world. If there are too many dating books on the market, why do millions of readers keep buying new books on the same subject? The answer is simple. People want new answers to solve their old problems.

How To Hook Up With And Date Beautiful Women offers different perspectives on casual sex, dating, romance, and love between men and women that you won't find in mainstream society. Writing a good book on hooking up and dating, which helps men conquer their fears and insecurities and get the sexual satisfaction they desire, could never be a waste of time. There simply aren't enough effective books on dating to accommodate every man, which is why there's always room on the shelf for one more.

Second, I've spoken at length with women who believe men should already know everything they need to know about the dating game when they meet them. I pointed out this was a rather unrealistic expectation, but they adamantly replied in dismissive tones that fathers are responsible for teaching their sons how to date.

The Washington Times ran a story about fathers disappearing from households across America on December 25, 2012, where fifteen million U.S. children, or 1 in 3, lived without a father. I pulled the story up on Google so the women could see the data for themselves.

I went to fatherhoodfactor.com whose first fatherless stat listed 23.6% of U.S. children (17.4 million) lived in father absent homes in 2014. I asked these women where 17.4 million fatherless young men were supposed to get good dating information if their fathers weren't present in their lives to teach them?

They replied men should have uncles, grandfathers, coaches from sports teams, deacons at church, or some other father figures in their lives willing to teach them how to date and treat women right. Their glib responses were steeped in denial, frustration, an indignant zeal to blame men, and they had zero interest in taking an impartial, analytical approach to examine this troubling issue with a critical eye.

I wasn't completely against what the women said because I believe fathers should teach their sons how to approach women for casual sex. However, these women made two mistakes. One, they assumed fathers have mastered the game to the point they can teach it to their sons. Two, they assumed fathers are willing to teach their sons the game. These women immediately took issue when I pointed out they were wrong on both counts.

Let me take this moment to set the record straight. If society had an abundance of men well-versed in the game, there wouldn't be so many dissatisfied women. There aren't enough fathers with tight game to teach their sons how to hook up with and date beautiful women on one hand, and there are fathers who don't teach their sons the game because they don't want their sons to become full-dog alpha males, ladies men, macks, players, and womanisers on the other.

My father never taught me the game, and it wasn't because he wasn't in my life. He's married to my mother, and he helped raise me from infancy to manhood, but he's a devout, evangelical Christian minister. And he's not one of these jackleg, phoney ass preachers perverting the Word of God for sex, money, and power.

He's an old school, holiness preacher who speaks out against sin and submits himself to the will of The Most High completely. I've seen him lay hands on people where The Most High healed them from terminal diseases. I've seen miracles. I'm not embellishing one word of this, and those who know me and my family personally know all of this to be true. My father walks with The Most High.

He's the perfect man to talk to if you're saved, you don't drink or smoke, you're not interested in dating and having casual sex with multiple women, and you're looking to get married and start a family. My father is an expert in marriage and relationship counselling, and he can give you time-tested advice and guidance that works.

But what if you're not saved? What if you're not interested in giving your life to the Lord and going to church at all? What if you just want to get high, get drunk, and fuck the shit out of beautiful women? What if that's all you want to do? My father wouldn't help you with any of that. In fact, he would talk to you about the spiritual downfalls of surrendering yourself to carnal lusts, and he would try to persuade you to abstain from sinful behaviour. What else would you expect from a true man of God?

My father never taught me how to approach women sexually. He taught me how to be respectful and conduct myself around women socially, which was great, but he never taught me how essential it was to flirt with women physically and verbally when I talked to them. He never taught me the significance of building sexual tension to the point where the woman's pussy gets wet, and she's ready to go back to the crib, get butt ass naked, and fuck.

My father is the greatest man I know, but he never taught me the game of getting women. Looking back now, I can understand why he didn't. We lived in the slums of southwest Detroit which was overrun with drug dealers, gangsters, and pimps, and he didn't want his children to idolise those men and adopt their cultures and criminal ways of life.

I see what he tried to do, and his heart was certainly in the right place, but his oversight became an unintentional failure to teach his sons how to approach women sexually, and this is a serious matter younger fathers with sons must address. If you're a father and you're not teaching your heterosexual son how to approach women for casual sex, you're doing him a disservice. He's going to get taken advantage of and played to perfection in the sexual marketplace.

There's an indeterminable percentage of men whose fathers taught them the game and how to carry themselves around women socially and sexually, but there's also an indeterminable percentage of men whose fathers, uncles, and grandfathers never taught them that. I'm one of those men.

I wouldn't be the man I am today without my father. I might not have escaped the slums of Detroit without his discipline, and the example of manhood he set for me. He tried his best to keep me on the straight and narrow path, and I fucked up royally despite his best efforts, but that's another story for another book. My father taught me a great deal, and I continue to learn from him today, but he never taught me how to approach women with charm and confidence to fuck them.

This is one area of development in a young man's life where he doesn't need a holiness preacher's guidance. Pre-marital sex is not a sin, and this is an area of human activity where young men need solid guidance and teaching from men who know how to approach beautiful women and have casual sex with them consistently.

There's a scarcity of men who possess tight game and sex appeal, and women know this better than most. They're the ones getting bombarded daily by thirsty men unschooled and unskilled in the game. They of all people should understand the lack of knowledge and the serious problem this presents. I wrote *How To Hook Up With And Date Beautiful Women* to bridge the gap and fill this crucial need.

Third, too many men and women dismiss the game as bullshit and assume men learn it so they can become players and womanisers. We're not going to spend too much time on ignorant misperceptions, but I'd like to clear the air.

When I use the term, "game," I'm referring to men who use charm, confidence, and straightforward, seductive talk to have casual sex with women without resorting to harassment, intimidation, violence, or paying for sexual favours. For those unfamiliar with the slang term, paying for sexual favours is known as "tricking" in the streets.

I don't condemn tricking for others because there are men who have to pay for sex. This is unfortunate, but life is real, and it is what it is. I won't begrudge those men their sexual satisfaction, and I won't deny sex workers their opportunities to make a living. Both parties win in those situations. No harm, no foul.

However, there's an indeterminable percentage of men tricking off their hard-earned money when they don't have to. Maybe you're one of those men. If this is the case, you will attract more women once you adjust your approach and learn game-proven and game-tested strategies to achieve your sexual goals.

The game doesn't turn men into players and womanisers. If a man learns the game, masters its principles, and uses his newfound knowledge to reinvent himself as a full-dog alpha male, ladies' man, mack, player, or womaniser, that's his choice, and he has to live with the consequences of his decision. I don't help men learn the game so they can become players and womanisers. I help men learn the game so they can master themselves and learn how to select the best women for them to approach and fuck. There's no deceit involved.

Fourth, what makes me an expert to write a book on casual sex and dating? I've walked through the fires of dealing with women for casual sex and dating and emerged as pure gold. I'm a self-taught authority with years of knowledge, practical experience, and skill.

I've won some, lost some, and learned from every conversation, tryst, short-term and long-term monogamous and non-monogamous relationship I've had with women. I've acquired insights from trial and error, studied how to turn rejection into strength, and learned how to separate the game from the truth.

This is why I have the confidence to go out by myself, meet a beautiful woman, flirt with her, build the essential sexual tension, and fuck her that night. Without tricking. Without taking her out on a date. Without promising monogamy.

Fifth, why did I write this book? I wrote *How To Hook Up With And Date Beautiful Women* because there's millions of men, many of them young and not so young anymore, who need game-tested, game-proven advice and instruction on how to approach women for hook ups or dates and have mind-blowing, spine-tingling, toe-curling sex with them. That's putting it nicely.

To be perfectly curt, there are millions of men in America, and millions more across the world who struggle to have sex. The majority of these men are afraid to approach the women they truly desire sexually because they don't know how, and they're terrified of rejection. This is particularly true if the women they desire are physically beautiful.

I perceive the size and scope of this enormous problem and offer this book as part of the solution. If fear and lack of confidence freeze you in your tracks as the women you desire pass you by, I couldn't be happier you're reading this. I'm here to help you build your confidence and realise your sexual potential. This is why I wrote *How To Hook Up With And Date Beautiful Women*. You're going to learn how to enjoy hook ups, dating, and get the sexual satisfaction you really want. This book is here to guide you, so take of the fruit of the game within its pages and eat.

CHAPTER 2

What Is Dating?

A romantic relationship is a three-act screenplay with a beginning, middle, and end. If it fails to gain the power and strength to last, it withers and dies in a breakup of some sort. Conversely, if a romantic relationship builds the power and strength to last, it becomes a love which lasts a lifetime. It becomes a precious, increasingly rare, emotional coupling between two human beings which ends with the death of one or both parties. Love always ends with someone leaving.

What is dating?

Dating is the beginning stage of romantic relationships where two people meet in order to determine each other's compatibility as potential partners in a sexual relationship or marriage.

It's changed forms with the passing of centuries, but it remains a form of courtship where couples enjoy social activities either alone, or in the company of others. It also involves people who already share romantic or sexual feelings for one another, which is why it's not uncommon for married couples to have date nights.

At its core, dating is how humans express their deep longing for intimacy and touch, and it has a remarkable history. Some of us are students of history who enjoy learning about human societies which existed before us and how they lived. Some of us enjoy history about as much as a root canal administered without any anaesthesia, so we'll only spend a brief moment on the history of dating.

Let's go way back in the day and return to ancient times when marriages began with raids and kidnappings. Whenever marriageable women grew scarce, warriors emboldened by horniness and the drive to create families raided neighbouring villages for wives. Nubile women were booty in the literal sense to be abducted and spirited away. Men from the bride's offended family and village inevitably came looking for her, which forced the thief and his stolen wife to go into hiding, and it doesn't take long for us to see how these bridal raids led to bloody skirmishes and wars between neighbouring societies.

Dating, as we know it today, wasn't a socially acceptable practise millennia ago. This goes back to a time when women were solely dependent on the goodwill of their fathers and husbands.

This goes back to a time when marriages in most societies were arranged by parents and older relatives, and they weren't centred around love and romance. At all. Arranged marriages were business relationships formed between families to build economic stability, political alliances, and strong legacies.

Marriage was exclusively for heterosexual couples at this time, and it was essentially a transaction which made wives a form of property exchanged between fathers and husbands with the explicit understanding women would provide healthy, able-bodied sons.

Marriages built upon business interests and political partnerships without love became prisons, and the unhappy husbands and wives locked inside them still longed for love and intimacy with the people they were unmistakably attracted to. These depressed men and women found the hot-blooded romance they craved in secret meetings with forbidden lovers outside of their marriages. These trysts were taboo and the vanguard to the dating scene we enjoy today.

Human societies have rigid attitudes which translate into equally rigid cultural, political and social practises when it comes to sex and marriage, so it took time for the iron grips of arranged marriages and parental influence to loosen a bit.

Centuries passed, and in the late 1800s, a new stage of courtship known as "calling" appeared in the Western world. Young men called on young women by visiting them in the parlours of their parents' homes. This represented a sea change in the courtship practises of the U.S. because this had never been done before.

The parents of young women supervised these meetings with watchful eyes, and the hopeful young men held themselves to the highest standards in order to make the best impressions possible. A young man's call was planned down to the last detail, which meant he knew when to arrive, how long to stay, and when to leave.

This type of parental supervision would be considered intrusive and invasive today, but it would deter many dishonourable men from raping and sexually assaulting women. This form of courtship also limited the opportunities for pre-marital sex, reduced the number of children born out of lawful wedlock, and gave parents much more time to get to know the men who wished to marry into their families.

Years rolled by, the late 1800s gave way to the 1900s, and courtship practises changed again, and the centre of courtship shifted away from calls in the family parlour under strict parental supervision to unmarried couples going out and socialising in public spaces. This was another significant development in the American courtship process which challenged parental control.

The Fifteenth U.S. Census, conducted by the Census Bureau one month from April 1, 1930, determined the resident population of the U.S. to be 123,202,624. The young men of courtship age who owned automobiles in 1930, enjoyed two luxuries which generations of young men who preceded them never had. The first was motorised mobility free from horse-drawn vehicles. The second was the freedom to take their young ladies of interest out on dates away from their homes.

Social calls in the family parlour which once served as the centre of courtship gave way to dining out at restaurants and dancing. Going to the movies. Attending plays. Going somewhere secluded, parking, drinking and doing whatever came next.

Those activities are nothing we think twice about today, but they represented another sea change in American courtship practises decades ago. The automobile moved the world forward in more ways than one.

The ascendance of the automobile created its own subculture where women showed the most sexual interest in the men who were rich enough to afford expensive cars and entertain them on dates which gave them a taste of the coveted good life.

Well-to-do men with money and fancy cars lavished their attention and time on the most physically attractive women who showed them the most sexual interest. The men with the money and fancy cars took pretty women on fun dates and expected sexual satisfaction in return. The pretty young women who cooperated fully were taken out on more dates, and the cycle continued. The women who refused this exchange got to spend their evenings at home in the family parlour with their siblings and parents.

The Sexual Revolution, also known as the time of Sexual Liberation, was a social movement which defied established conservative norms of sexuality and romantic relationships from the 1960s to the 1980s. The insuppressible, runaway power of the Sexual Revolution shook mainstream, white-bread America, western Europe, parts of Asia, and produced an international paradigm shift in attitudes toward the freedom of sexual expression, homosexuality, premarital sexuality, and women's sexuality.

This global change in thinking led to widespread acceptance of sex outside of heterosexual monogamous relationships and marriage, which had always been the norm. The Sexual Revolution reached critical mass and exploded into an entirely new set of norms which included the acceptance of contraception, the birth control pill, homosexuality, pornography, premarital sex, and public nudity.

Dating and casual sex became the new normal in the 1970s, and this represented yet another sea change. Abortion was legalised in 1973, no-fault divorces were legalised in 1974, and the birth control pill was made available to the public.

All of these contributing factors made it much easier for people to have sex outside of marriage without fearing the consequences of unwanted pregnancies (as much). Some would argue the Sexual Revolution continues today with the rise of transgenders and their struggle for acceptance and equality.

This concludes my brief history lesson on courtship and dating. I want to give my discouraged, frustrated brethren a different perspective on women, sex, and themselves because incessant social programming has led an indeterminable segment of them to mask their insecurities about women and hide from their fears of rejection instead of confronting and overcoming them.

There is no shame in feeling fear. When you see a beautiful woman and icy fear wraps itself around your balls, there are millions of other men who feel that same emotion. Fear is the dividing line in the game which separates the men who have casual sex with women from those who don't.

The men who confront and overcome their fear of rejection will approach women for casual sex. They're not going to be successful with all of the women they talk to, but they're going to have sex with some of the women they approach. It's a numbers game where the sex can remain casual or develop into short-term monogamy, long-term monogamy, or marriage. The men who master their fear of rejection and approach women have much better chances to experience sexual satisfaction.

Conversely, the men who fail to overcome their fear of rejection from women and refuse to learn the game tend to blame women for their inability to face this debilitating fear. They also blame men who seduce and have sex with women.

These men use others as scapegoats and refuse to accept any personal responsibility for their weak ass game. They delude themselves and hope against hope the next day will be different, but that day never arrives because they refuse to improve themselves and learn the game which would help them attract the beautiful women they desire.

A man's refusal to confront his fear of rejection creates sexual frustration. His unrelieved sexual frustration turns into anger where he blames women, as well as the men who have casual sex with women for his own inability to do the same. His unrelieved sexual frustration, internalised anger, and envy then twists and turns into hatred and thoughts of violence which can lead him down a dark, deadly path.

There's an indeterminable segment of the world's male population who refer to themselves as incels. Incel is short for involuntary celibate. The incel subculture appears to consist of online communities defined by members unable to find romantic or sexual partners, and they describe this state of being as involuntary celibacy.

Chats in incel forums tend to revolve around bitterness, misogyny, and green-lighting the use of violence against women and the men who have sex with women. Incels describe this ideology as taking the black pill. The misogynistic, racist and violent language of incel communities led to them being banned from several web hosts and websites which was bad enough, but there have also been several mass murders committed by men who either identified themselves as incels or aligned themselves with incel ideologies.

I included a snapshot on the history of dating to show my discouraged, frustrated brethren they don't have that much to complain about. They have every reason to celebrate actually, but they fail to see this because they choose to remain focused on their past failures and cleave to their deep-seated anger, bitterness, and hatred of women. What my discouraged, frustrated brethren fail to realise is there has never been any other point in history where men in the Western world have lived in such sexually permissive times as those we enjoy today.

Healthy, single, able-bodied men in Western societies are free to fuck as many women as they want, and this sexual freedom is historically unprecedented. There are millions upon millions of women who like having casual sex, so why do so many men continue to struggle? The answer is four-pronged.

First, there's an indeterminable percentage of men who cleave to their deep-rooted anger, bitterness, and violent impulses they harbour toward women. If we want to gain a clearer understanding of their misogynistic behaviour, we have to place their conduct in the proper sociohistorical context, and analyse the circumstances which continue to produce sexism and a fervent hatred of women deep within the hearts, minds, and spirits of an indeterminable segment of the male population in the U.S. which certainly appears to be the majority.

Sexism is an integral part of America's culture and always has been. Some Americans have the decency and honesty to admit this while too many others choose to delude themselves and live in denial.

When the Pilgrim Fathers built the first English colonial society in Jamestown, Virginia, in 1607, and then another in New Plymouth, Massachusetts, in 1620, they built societies with institutions and laws that favoured and protected wealthy white Christian male landowners.

Those were the upper class men most favoured in England where they came from, this was the culture they were accustomed to, so they brought their classist, racist and sexist beliefs and cultural practises across the Atlantic Ocean with them. People bring their culture with them when they move from one place to another because it's their way of life. It's all they know, and this is why sexism is as American as baseball, apple pie, and school shootings.

The behaviour based on traditional stereotypes of gender roles, gender-based discrimination, and ingrained, institutionalised prejudice against women has been passed down for generations since the 17th century, and this has led an indeterminable segment of the male population in the U.S. to believe women are inferior beings who owe them sex. The problem is compounded because this belief in male entitlement is normalised in society, and constantly reinforced in pop culture through comic books, graphic novels, films, novels, songs, TV shows, and video games.

The underlying messages which suggest men are entitled to fuck women and women should submit to their sexual advances are pushed to male and female audiences alike. The influence of pop culture is far-reaching, and its impact helps construct our world and mould our perception of reality.

So what happens when men who believe women owe them sex approach women who reject them? Rejection is the nature of the game, but their ridiculous sense of entitlement blinds them to this, so these men take offence instead of taking rejection in stride and moving on.

Some men verbally abuse women who reject them, others lash out and attack women physically, and then we have men who take such offence at being rejected sexually they murder the women who don't want them. Women have their ways of determining a man's vibe, and once they feel a man is an angry, arrogant, bitter douchebag who could possibly become violent, they're not going to be interested in having casual sex with him.

Casual sex isn't going to happen, dating isn't going to happen, and platonic friendship isn't going to happen either because women have no use for those kinds of men.

You aren't entitled to sex. Your sense of entitlement is bullshit, it's dangerous, and it's not going to help you fuck the women you desire. I encourage you to change the way you think about women, sex, and yourself, and if you aren't sure how to do this keep reading. I will show you the way.

Second, we have an indeterminable percentage of men who refuse to improve themselves in ways which will make them more attractive to women. Humans are narcissistic to varying degrees, so it's natural for people to resist criticism on some level. I understand this, but you can't argue with results, and if you aren't attracting the women you desire, then you need to look inward to find the root(s) of your problem(s).

Do you need to change your personal hygiene? Do you need to change how you dress and adopt a sexier style? Do you need to improve your confidence, and grow the backbone and balls required to approach women and seduce them?

You know where your weaknesses lie and blaming women and other men for your deficiencies isn't going to help you hook up with and date beautiful women. Not unless you're one hell of a comedian who can take his rants about rejection and his refusal to change and turn that material into priceless stand-up comedy routines which could lead to a Netflix deal.

If you aren't that funny (and most of us aren't), I encourage you to look inward and address your deficiencies. Learn to make yourself strong where you're weak. There are millions upon millions of women in America who have zero problems having casual sex, so if women aren't interested in fucking you, humble yourself, find the flaws in your game and fix them. Turn your weaknesses into strengths. Humble yourself, learn the game, and make yourself more attractive to women in general.

Anger, bitterness, and resentment don't help you hook up with and date beautiful women. Refusing to improve your game doesn't help your cause either. Women don't owe you sex, nor are they obligated to find you attractive. If you want to have casual sex or find a girlfriend or wife to share your love and life's loneliness with, it's your responsibility to make yourself the most attractive man you can be. If you aren't sure how to do that, keep reading. I will show you the way.

Third, we have men with fragile egos who cannot accept rejection from women. Rejection hurts and cuts to the quick without breaking skin and bone or spilling a drop of blood. Rejection can make a man angry enough to commit murder.

According to an article written by Olga Khazan on July 20, 2017, the Centres for Disease Control and Prevention released a report which proved over half of the killings of American women were related to intimate partner violence where the vast majority of the victims died after being attacked by a current or former romantic partner. Male rage is real, and it ends the lives of hundreds of women every year.

Perhaps my discouraged, frustrated, murderous brethren aren't aware of this or perhaps they simply don't give a fuck at this point, but nearly every heterosexual male experiences rejection from women at some point in his life. It's our common ground as heterosexual men because nearly all of us have been turned down by women we wanted. No one likes rejection. The shit sucks, but no man has the right to mistreat or murder a woman because she doesn't want to have sex with him.

A study released by the Violence Policy Centre on September 20, 2016, revealed more than 1,600 women were murdered by men in 2014 who couldn't just move on, and the most common weapon used was a gun. The data is chilling. Nationwide, 1,613 females were killed by males in single victim/single offender incidents in 2014, at a rate of 1.08 per 100,000.

The study found that ninety-three percent of women killed by men were murdered by someone they knew. Of the victims who knew their offenders, sixty-three percent were wives or other intimate acquaintances of their killers. Thirteen times as many females were murdered by a male they knew than were killed by male strangers. One thousand, six hundred and thirteen women lost their lives to men with frail egos who were too weak to accept rejection and move on with their lives.

Those were needless murders and women are well aware former lovers can become homicidal after they've been dumped. How can a battered woman leave an abusive relationship when she gathers the strength to walk away only to have her ex-boyfriend or ex-husband break into her new home and gun her down? If women get the feeling you might become violent with them, they aren't going to want to be around you, your negative energy, or the very real threat you could pose to their lives. Not unless they're accustomed to being with violent, abusive men.

Women don't have to date you, have sex with you, or be around you just to soothe your ego. If you want to have casual sex with beautiful women or date them, you have to strengthen your resolve and develop sufficient backbone and balls where you can accept rejection, take it in stride, and move on to approach other beautiful women without flying into a rage and killing someone. If you aren't sure how to do this, keep reading. I will show you the way.

Fourth, we have men who refuse to understand sexual deception and the true nature of women. If you refuse to acknowledge, understand, and accept that many if not most women are sexually deceptive, you will fail to understand the true nature of the women you want to deal with. You won't be able to have casual sex or date them successfully, and you won't grow in the game. You will fall flat on your fucking face. Let's move on to the next chapter, where we will cover sexual deception and the true nature of women in more detail.

15 MAY 18 (TUE)
1313/Kokio Chicken
Koreatown, Los Angeles, California

CHAPTER 3

Understanding Sexual Deception And The True Nature Of Women

There's an indeterminable segment of the male and female populations in the U.S. who lie and practise deception. There are boys, girls, men, and women who lie as easily as they breathe. Sex is an area of human activity where deceptive people cloak their real intentions and true natures behind well-maintained façades and plastic smiles in order to get what they want.

If you have little to no sexual experience with women, learning the game is a must. If you want to have casual sex with multiple women consistently, you have to understand sexual deception and the true nature of women.

Deceit is a noun defined as the action or practise of deceiving and concealing the truth in order to mislead. Whenever men and women are being deceptive, they're practising the art of concealing the truth in order to mislead one or more people.

Let's take a look at Rick, a successful twenty-eight-year-old entertainment attorney from Pacific Palisades, a coastal neighbourhood on the Los Angeles Westside. Married for four years with a son and daughter, he is the epitome of a loving husband, father, and family man in the eyes and minds of his business associates, co-workers, family, friends, and peers.

Things are not always as they seem, however, and the first appearance deceives many as Phaedrus once said. Rick is not so happily married, and he's having extramarital affairs with comely fuck buddies in Atlanta, Chicago, Miami, and New York City. He flies out of town on business regularly, so frequent travel helps him stay connected with his whores.

Rick would never take his wedding ring off in front of his wife, family, friends, or co-workers because this would raise questions and create juicy chatter about the stability of his marriage behind his back, so he takes his wedding band off in the backseat of the autonomous taxi on his way to LAX.

His wife has no idea he's cheating on her, and his mistresses don't know he's married. Rick practises deceit when he takes his wedding ring off because he misleads women into believing he's single when he's not. He has no problem lying to women in order to have casual sex with them, and he has no problem lying to his wife in order to keep his home secure. This makes Rick a sexually deceptive man.

Let's take a look at Athena, a shapely nineteen-year-old woman and Olympic hopeful from the Crenshaw District in South Los Angeles. A sophomore track and field sprinter at the University of Southern California, she likes cannabis, working out, walks on the beach, going to Dodgers, Lakers and Rams games, Kokio chicken, and anal sex (with the right partners).

I'm not a fan of the one to ten scale of sexual attractiveness because it's subjective. Beauty is in the eye of the beholder, so the numbers aren't going to be universal across the board. However, the one to ten scale is a ranking system large masses of people can conceptualise and understand, so let's say Athena's body is a ten.

She works out, trains religiously, and the results are stunning. Men stop and stare at her bubble ass, slim waist, sculpted calves and thighs, and D-cup tits which stand at attention like

U.S. Marines undergoing in-quarters inspection. The beauty of her perfect body, however, is offset by her face, which is a six. She has supreme confidence in her body, but she harbours insecurities about her less than perfect face.

She's in love with Alan, a popular pretty boy, starting power forward on the Trojans basketball team, and member of Kappa Alpha Psi Fraternity Incorporated. Alan is swimming in pussy. He barely knows Athena is alive, and he treats her like shit truth be told, but she has multiple orgasms whenever he makes time to fuck her.

She knows Alan is a player. She knows he will never be anything more than an easy smile in her face, dirty talk in her ear, and a long, hard, black dick in her ass, mouth, and pussy, but she cannot leave the hard-partying, college basketball star alone. She tried. Many times. But ultimately, she was unable to resist his womanising aura, full-dog alpha male energy, and thoroughly satisfying manner of rough sex.

She keeps Alan in her life because he's the most attractive man in her dating pool, he gives her the best sex she's ever had, he's a frat boy she likes partying with, and he's a projected lottery pick in the upcoming NBA Draft. They met at a beach party in Malibu after the USC-Oregon game where she sucked his dick, swallowed his seed, and fucked him the same night she met him. Keep that in mind, okay?

Athena met Robert at the Museum of Contemporary Art, Los Angeles last week. He's a sophomore who smokes weed, plays guitar, operates his own non-profit organisation to feed the homeless on Skid Row, and carries a perfect 4.0 grade point average in USC's undergraduate pre-med program. He plans to attend medical school at Harvard University.

Alan is a full-dog alpha male. A player with swagger on and off the court, he isn't remotely interested in anything other than working out, playing ball in the NBA, buying franchises, investing wisely in the stock market to build his wealth, and having casual sex with the most beautiful women he can find.

Robert is not a full-dog alpha male. He attracts women interested in casual sex, long-term monogamous relationships which could lead to marriage, and short-term to long-term polyamorous relationships (non-monogamous sex) or extramarital affairs. He comes from a well-to-do family in Chicago's North Shore, he's a genius, he's going to be a Harvard educated surgeon, and he's what women refer to as boyfriend material.

Alan barely makes time for her now, so Athena knows she probably won't see him again after he gets drafted into the NBA. She can't see a future for herself with the man she truly desires, but Robert is a great consolation prize. She sees Robert as boyfriend material, who will make an excellent father and husband, she wants to get her hooks in him early, so she isn't going to risk losing him by giving him the pussy too soon.

They haven't gone out yet, but she's already decided to withhold sex from him until their third or fourth date because she doesn't want him to see her as a sexually promiscuous slut. Experience has taught the young runner that high-quality men like to have sex with the women they see as sluts and whores, but they don't like to marry them.

Athena didn't withhold sex from Alan to earn his respect. She sucked his dick and fucked him fifteen minutes after she met him. She had no problem being sexually promiscuous and completely uninhibited with the womanising frat boy and a few of his teammates. She didn't make them wait for sex, but she's definitely going to make Robert wait.

She's going to carry herself like a sexually conservative woman who practises monogamy, and that isn't who she is. At all. She's presenting herself as someone she isn't to mislead Robert into respecting her and making her his girlfriend. She has no problem concealing her true sexual nature in order to secure a long-term monogamous relationship with a man who's going to be rich and powerful in the future. This is fraudulent, self-serving behaviour which makes Athena a sexually deceptive woman.

Before the year 1960, dating in the U.S. centred around heterosexual men and women entering into long-term monogamous romantic relationships which led to marriage. There were people and couples who weren't heterosexual, and they were marginalised because bisexuality, homosexuality, lesbianism, pansexuality, and transgenderism weren't tolerated in white mainstream society then.

We covered this briefly in chapter two when we looked at the history of dating, but it bears revisiting because the austere conservatism which ruled America before 1960, the social movements which defied and disrupted authority on every level during the 1960s and 70s, and the subsequent upheavals which pushed society forward and completely transformed dating and courtship practises provide the proper historical context for us to better interpret and navigate the dating and courtship culture of today.

The conservatism which ruled America prior to the year 1960 reaches back to a time when young men were expected to marry their high school sweethearts or college sweethearts, create families, and they did so in great numbers. This conservatism reaches back to a time when women didn't have casual sex nearly as much as they do now, and men dated women who remained virgins until the day they were wed. This conservatism reaches back to a time when unmarried women were disowned for having children out of wedlock.

We aren't going to look back on this chapter of history with rose-coloured glasses. Then as now, there were couples who withered in dispirited marriages. Then as now, there were husbands and wives who betrayed their spouses and indulged in extramarital affairs. We aren't going to look back at the people from those times with rose-coloured glasses either.

Then as now, men accuse women of being more sexually deceptive than they are and vice versa. This is a fruitless debate with no end, and here's the truth behind the finger pointing: indeterminable segments of the male and female human populations are sexually deceptive and always have been.

Historically, men have always had more freedom to be sexually deceptive than women. Then the rapid ascent of feminism and the establishment-smashing tsunami of the Sexual Revolution shook the 1960s and 70s like rag dolls in a Miami hurricane.

After the dust settled, American women found themselves with a brand new set of fun, shiny tools: the combined oral contraceptive pill known much more commonly as the birth control pill, no-fault divorce, and legalised abortion. There's an indeterminable percentage of women who have always been sexually deceptive, but they were constrained by society and their own bodies from acting on their lustful, underhanded impulses and instincts in ways men were not.

Before 1960, unmarried women might have been much more hesitant to have casual sex because they didn't have birth control pills. They hadn't been invented yet, so a mistake during ecstasy had a much higher probability of turning into an unwanted pregnancy. Society was far more conservative then, so if a young, unmarried woman got pregnant, her parents might have forced her to marry the child's father.

Before 1960, there were married women who were ill at ease having sex with their husbands at times for fear of pregnancies which would strain their finances. So imagine the miraculous delight, relief, and wonder American women felt when they were given the power to control their pregnancies, end their marriages without proving any fault on the parts of their spouses, and end their unwanted pregnancies.

They suddenly had life-changing power previous generations of wives and mothers could only dream of, and this newfound power gave sexually deceptive women the freedom to act on their lustful, duplicitous instincts.

So what is the nature of women?

Human nature has prosocial and selfish traits alike, so women cooperate with others when it suits their needs, and they become selfish when selfishness serves them best. Men are no different. We do what's in our best interests as well, so I find it amusing when my brethren complain about the ways of women which aren't all that different from the ways of men. The average man seeks to please himself first and foremost, and the average woman is no different in that respect.

The true nature of an indeterminable percentage of women from the West leads them to be sexually deceptive and secure their own needs first. This makes sense given how Western culture was built upon men dominating women in all ten areas of human activity which include crime, economics, education, entertainment, labour, law, politics, religion, sex, and war.

Men held the upper hand for millennia, and they grew accustomed to the power and control they held over women's lives. This power corrupted them, and they forced monogamy upon women while they reserved the right to be promiscuous and have concubines and mistresses for themselves.

Men had their cake and eat it too, and they enjoyed having it both ways until feminism and the Sexual Revolution exploded on American soil, and posed a lethal threat to their established patriarchy. The birth control pill, no-fault divorce, and legalised abortion snapped much of men's control over women's reproductive rights in half like brittle twigs, gave women unprecedented power, and the indeterminable segment of sexually deceptive women have used their autonomy to have their cake and eat it too along with a tall, ice-cold glass of milk ever since.

Women know the power of the pussy, they know men are weak for sex, and they use their power to have it both ways. This isn't to suggest all women are sexually deceptive because an indeterminable percentage of them practise monogamy. This percentage can't be measured accurately because human beings can't be relied upon to be completely honest, but there are women who will only be intimate and have sex with their long-term monogamous boyfriends, fiancés, and husbands.

My cousin, M.K., abstained from premarital sex until her wedding day. She was a pretty twenty-four-year-old who men tried to seduce on a regular basis, so how was she able to turn all of them down, reject their advances, and remain pure for her husband on their wedding night?

She's a devout Christian with unshakeable faith. This may be hard for some readers to believe, but there really are women with unyielding religious faith who shun promiscuity and abstain from sex until they get married. If you're a man who wants to enjoy casual sex with multiple comely women, don't try to seduce women with deep, abiding religious faith.

You have a much better chance of seducing women who are already having casual sex, but they tend to practise sexual deception because they like having it both ways. They want their cake, eat it too, and a tall, ice-cold glass of milk on the side. Just like men do. Sexually deceptive women select three types of men to serve them.

1. Fuck buddies. Sexually deceptive women prefer to have casual sex with full-dog alpha males, ladies' men, macks, players, and womanisers. There are no delusions of love or romance in fuck buddy pairings. Full-dog alpha males, ladies' men, macks, players, and womanisers aren't taking women out on dates, but they're definitely fucking the women they desire.

In every hole.

Women don't flake on their fuck buddies. They flake on guys they don't really like sexually. If you want to see where you stand in the game and determine your sexual marketplace value, think back to the last time a woman flaked on you. Did she cancel for a legitimate reason? Or do you think she blew you off to go lick the balls and ride the dick of one of her fuck buddies?

2. Companions. Sexually deceptive women select certain men for companionship, and I refer to these men as boyfriend material and sponsors respectively. They tend to be either full-dog alpha males who fell in love, or they're former simps who strengthened their backbones, grew some balls, and developed the confidence to be straightforward with women about casual sex.

Men classified as boyfriend material appeal to women interested in long-term monogamous relationships which could lead to marriage, and women interested in long-term non-monogamous (polyamorous) sex or extramarital affairs. Sponsors appeal to women after they offer to provide a degree of access to their finances and bottomless monogamy. If they didn't offer women money and devotion, they wouldn't get women.

Full-dog alpha males, ladies' men, macks, players, and womanisers are women's first choice for fuck buddies, and this frustrates an indeterminable percentage of men to no end. The men classified as boyfriend material, are women's first choice for long-term romantic companionship. If women are unable to secure the boyfriend material they truly desire, the sponsors become suitable second place prizes. In fact, an indeterminable percentage of women prefer sponsors, because they're willing to spend money and they're easily controlled.

3. Simpletons. Scheming women select certain men to be their simpletons. Also known as cucks, inches, male girlfriends, simps, and white knights, these men grew up being bullied, harassed, and intimidated by their parents, siblings, friends, and classmates alike through childhood, adolescence, and adulthood. They never developed the confidence and courage to overcome their fears, stand up to bullies, and defend themselves.

Simps become weak-willed men as a result of this conditioning. And while their brown-nosing and timidity turn women off sexually, there's an indeterminable segment of women who love dominating men's attention and non-sexual time even though they have no real intentions on ever becoming the girlfriends and wives of the men they exploit. An indeterminable percentage of women adore having simpletons fawning over them and spending money on them while they have nothing but contempt and mockery for those men in their hearts.

Perhaps your parent(s) never took the time to explain the grim facts of life to you. Perhaps you never had a pimp or an older, experienced, true-to-the-game player pull your coat and lace you with some iceberg game, but there are millions upon millions of women who are cruel enough to deceive you, use you for everything they can for as long as they can, then kick you over the curb like garbage without a second thought. Many simps grow enraged at the deceptive women they allowed to exploit them and thirst for blood and murder.

This is understandable because it's human nature to place blame on others for one's mistakes. I've done it before, chances are you have too at some point in your life, and women who mistreat men and abandon them in such cutthroat fashion are certainly not innocent, but at the end of the day, simps have no one to blame but themselves.

If you place your full trust in another human being when it comes to money, romance, and sex, you're a goddamn fool.

Human beings are the most deceptive, self-destructive, selfish, and violent species on Earth. No amount of love and devotion will change basic human instincts, so if you ever place your full trust in another man or woman, you're a muthafucking fool, and you have no one to blame but yourself. This is the way of the world, and it is what it is. Consider yourself warned.

4. Untouchables. There's an indeterminable segment of the male population women have zero interest in. I refer to these unfortunate folks are the untouchables. Women don't want attention, companionship, money, platonic friendship, or sex from them. Women don't want anything from these men, and they want nothing to do with them. At all. The untouchables are sexually invisible in the eyes of women the way unattractive women are virtually invisible in the eyes of men on the prowl for beautiful women.

The Failings Of Each Class:

1. Fuck buddies. Full-dog alpha males, ladies' men, macks, players, and womanisers have the charm, charisma, raw sexuality, and utter indifference to turn women all the way on and get their pussies wet. This is why women choose them to be their fuck buddies. These men get an overabundance of pussy because an overabundance of women, single and married alike, enjoy having short-term non-monogamous sex with them.

The men in the fuck buddy class are aloof, and sex-fuelled hubris clouds their judgment. Full-dog alpha males perceive women as sexual conquests. Their energy attracts women who want to have casual sex in waves, but it also alienates women with wifely ambitions and exceptional motherly qualities who want to create loving, long-term monogamous relationships and have children.

Unhappy women in long-term relationships, engagements, and marriages prefer full-dog alpha males as their back door men, and that role is always open for them. However, more than a few full-dog alpha males find themselves seeking healthy, long-term, monogamous relationships in their mid to late thirties, forties, and fifties because they failed to recognise and choose the sterling quality women who would have gladly become their wives and the mothers of their children.

If you're a man in the fuck buddy class and you have absolutely no desire to get married and start a family, feel free to disregard this passage. Continue fucking the women in your life left, right, front, back, and side to side. You're good to go. Conversely, if you're a man in the fuck buddy class with a desire to marry and start a family, don't wait until you're thirty-five years of age or older to get started.

Time and tide wait for no man. Start looking for your wife and mother of your children when you feel the stirrings to settle down. Look for comely women who want to get married and create families, and see what they have to offer you beyond bubble asses, baby-making hips, juicy vaginas, and luscious, dick sucking lips.

An indeterminable percentage of men in the fuck buddy class fail to give the right opportunities to the right women at the right times in their lives because they're so preoccupied with casual sex, they reduce their potential wives to inconsequential pieces of ass. This is how they bypass the women who could help make their lives more fulfilled. If you're a full-dog alpha male, ladies' man, mack, player, or womaniser with a desire to marry and create your own family, you want to avoid this pitfall and succeed where so many others in your class have failed miserably.

2. Companions. The men classified as boyfriend material and sponsors sit comfortably in the companions class. The men with boyfriend material are more attractive to women than full-dog alpha males, sponsors, and untouchables because they appeal to women who want long-term monogamous relationships which will lead to marriage, as well as other women who want long-term polyamorous sexcapades or thoroughly satisfying extramarital affairs.

Sponsors don't elicit these responses from women. Sponsors appeal to women after they offer to provide them with financial support and bottomless monogamy whether that be in a short-term relationship, long-term relationship, or marriage.

They're never the top options on women's list of most desirable sex partners, but an indeterminable percentage of women deal with sponsors because they offer real financial support in exchange for a façade of love, and they're easily controlled in romantic relationships due to their complete lack of balls, backbone, and confidence. Sponsors don't stand up for themselves, and they don't present any sort of challenge to women. This is why they fail.

The men with boyfriend material fail because they appeal to so many women sexually. They attract women who want long-term monogamous relationships as well as other women who prefer booty calls, weekend flings, and non-monogamous sexcapades in general. The men considered to be boyfriend material may be strong, upstanding men with charisma and leadership qualities, but they're still men with an innate weakness for beautiful women and pussy. They aren't above practising sexual deception when they feel they can get away with it.

An indeterminable segment of the men considered to be boyfriend material will happily cheat on their girlfriends, fiancées, and wives by concealing their long-term monogamous relationships and marriages from the women they want to have casual sex with. They will do this whenever it suits them best because they lust after the pussy as sexually active heterosexual men are wont to do.

An indeterminable segment of the female population know the boyfriend material men they're dealing with are already in long-term relationships or married, yet they fuck these men anyway. These women are deceitful, they want to enjoy thoroughly satisfying sex, and they lust after men with good dick and tight game as sexually active heterosexual women are wont to do. If you're a man considered to be boyfriend material or a sponsor, you want to avoid those pitfalls and succeed where so many others in your class have failed miserably.

3. Simpletons and Untouchables. Simps have a deplorable choice to make: either remain invisible in the eyes of the comely women they want to fuck or enjoy being their trusty emotional tampons.

This is a lose-lose situation because men don't want to be ignored by the women they're interested in, nor do they want to waste their invaluable time flattering and wheedling women, and stooping low enough to listen to these silly, conniving bitches complain, cry, and long for the full-dog alpha males and men with boyfriend material who fucked them, dogged the shit out of them, and left them feeling abandoned, angry, brokenhearted, and disillusioned without getting so much as a kiss or some decent oral sex in return.

Fellatio is an acceptable form of currency for relationship therapy, but sex of any sort is out of the question because women have zero interest in fucking simps and untouchables. Simps and untouchables masturbate and support sex workers. They pay for that peculiar feeling between love and loneliness. This is another lose-lose situation. This is the bitter root of the sexual frustration which chokes the joy out of their lives.

Simps are conditioned to believe physically beautiful women are to be adored, praised and protected at all costs, but they lack the confidence to approach the women they desire for casual sex and dates. They want beautiful, long-term monogamous girlfriends and wives, and they don't have a snowball's chance in Hell of making this happen, but they pander to these women anyway. They accommodate them at every turn out of desperation to have some sort of female companionship in their lives.

Deceptive women pick up on this immediately and string these lonely bastards along for weeks, months, and even years in some instances with false hopes in exchange for attention, money, and non-sexual time. Simps and crafty women play this sad game of cat and mouse with each other for weeks, months and years in some cases until it plays out which leaves the simps sick at heart, cast adrift in a sea of loneliness.

The trouble starts when simps realise they never go out on dates or have sex with the women they want to fuck. They realise they've never had any romantic moments with the women they truly desire. If they're not virgins which is a long shot, they realise all of their orgasms come from masturbation inspired by porn or sex workers.

The horrible truth of their simpleton status finally dawns upon them, and they grasp what should have been obvious the whole time: women don't want to have sex with them. Women don't enjoy their non-sexual companionship. Women have no desire to be around them. Simps don't have loving girlfriends, devoted wives or strong families in their futures.

These life-shattering realisations leave an indeterminable segment of the simp population brokenhearted. The women they worshipped abandoned them to date, marry, and have the child(ren) of full-dog alpha males and men with boyfriend material. The betrayal adds insult to injury and pours salt into deep, raw emotional wounds. The hypocrisy and irony of these situations aren't lost on an indeterminable percentage of the simpletons who start to understand just how badly they were used. These dejected men understand they allowed women to exploit their desperation, foolishness, gullibility, and lack of game, and they place the blame where it lies, which is squarely upon their own shoulders.

Accepting personal responsibility for their shortcomings allows this percentage of simps to identify their weaknesses, improve their strengths, learn the game, and become men considered boyfriend material. Some might find this hard to believe, but it doesn't change the fact people can change for the better. All it takes is commitment, effort, motivation, and tenacity.

There's another indeterminable segment of the simp population, however, who refuse to hold themselves accountable for how they allowed women to play them. They place one hundred percent of their blame and anger on the women who exploited them. Their anger and sexual frustration turns into embittered misogyny and unvented rage directed against women in general.

The devotion, love, and respect they held for women mutates into cold abhorrence and a quenchless thirst for revenge and violence. Some might find this hard to believe, but it doesn't change the fact people can change for the worse. All it takes is commitment, effort, motivation, and tenacity.

This is the black pill process through which an indeterminable segment of the simpleton population completes the metamorphosis from emotional tampons to full-blown, women-hating homicidal simps and incels who attack women in word and deed. This is how an indeterminable segment of simps degenerate into mass murderers, serial killers, and serial rapists who will gladly kill women and the men who appeal to them sexually.

Why do homicidal simps and incels feel compelled to murder men right alongside women? They know they have zero chance of competing against full-dog alpha males and the men with boyfriend material for women's affection, companionship, and love which is what they seek above all else. Homicidal simps and incels abhor the women they cannot have sexually, the men who are able to have sex with women, and they don't have any problem attacking either gender verbally and physically.

Homicidal simps and incels have no qualms and little to no remorse about lashing out violently with lethal force against people who may or may not have offended them, because they've repressed so much of their embittered misogyny and unvented rage they've lost touch with reality. Anger, bitterness, and hatred are powerful, destructive emotions which have to be released, or they feed upon the host like rapacious parasites until the host is consumed.

Then the grim day of reckoning arrives when a homicidal simp or incel can contain his toxic sensibilities no longer, he lashes out with knives, guns, and whatever else he can get his hands on, and yet another senseless, mass murder-suicide fuelled by racism, rage, a fervent hatred of women, and maddening sexual frustration makes the news cycle. Again. And America looks like a fucking shithole of a crumbling Western society gone mad overrun with bloodthirsty, gun-coveting, death-worshipping savages who cannot enjoy life without killing people. Again.

This should come as no surprise to Americans. Especially since no other industrialised country comes close to having the rate of gun violence we experience here. According to an article written by Sam Morris and the Guardian US interactive team for the guardian.com on February 15, 2018, Americans own an estimated 265 million guns which is more than one firearm for every adult.

Data from the Gun Violence Archive shows there's a mass shooting which is defined as four or more people shot in one incident (not including the shooter) nine out of every ten days on average. Simpletons fail when they refuse to accept any personal responsibility for allowing the women they desire to manipulate and deceive them.

The women aren't blameless, but if a man is naive enough to allow women to mistreat him repeatedly, he's no longer a victim. He's a volunteer with no one else to blame but himself. Simpletons fail when they succumb to their anger, misogyny, and envy of men desired by women.

There are simps who don't harm or kill others, but they fail when they normalise a lifestyle of masturbation, porn, impersonal orgasms with sex workers, and a love life devoid of genuine intimacy with the women they want to love and receive love from in return. Unfortunately, the men in the untouchables class are never going to seduce and have casual sex with the women they desire. There are different reasons for this, and those circumstances cannot be helped.

If you're a man in the simpleton class, you want to avoid these pitfalls, succeed where others in your class have failed miserably, and you might be able to do this. There might be a dot of light at the end of your tunnel. I can't make any guarantees, and I don't want to create any false expectations, but I invite you to visit my blog at www.westcoastwriter.com and contact me for a consultation where we can determine if I can help you make the necessary changes in how you perceive yourself, women, love, and sex.

The women you desire are having sex. They're just not having sex with you. The women you desire are going out on dates. They're just not dating you. There may be more than one reason for this, so let's see if we can put our heads together and find a solution.

29 MAY 18 (TUES)
1437/Hurricane Tax
Koreatown, Los Angeles, California

CHAPTER 4

You Don't Have To Take Women Out On Dates In Order To Fuck Them

The title of this chapter may throw you off because it defies the defective social programming you've been conditioned to accept and normalise, but you don't have to take women out on dates in order to fuck them. In fact, contrary to popular belief, if you want to hook up with beautiful women for casual sex and you're not interested in having short-term or long-term monogamous relationships with them, you shouldn't take them out on dates at all.

This chapter alone makes *How to Hook Up With And Date Beautiful Women* worth far more than the money you paid for it. How is that possible? You're going to learn how to use two of your most precious resources, your time and money, much more efficiently in your sexual dealings with women. If you read this book, comprehend its principles, and practise the game on a daily basis, you're going to learn how to stop wasting your time and money on pursuing women who don't want to have casual sex with you.

There are legions of hapless men, thoroughly unschooled and unskilled in the game, who waste thousands of dollars and countless hours which add up to weeks, months, and years pursuing women who have zero interest in dating or having casual sex with them. These are some profoundly unhappy muthafuckas, and I don't want you to fall into their broken ranks. That's why I wrote this book.

If all you want from beautiful women is casual sex, don't take them out on dates to dinner and the movies. Don't take women to concerts, museums, plays, or long walks in the park either. There aren't going to be any walks in the park. Don't have extended texting sessions and long conversations on the phone with them.

If all you truly want from beautiful women is casual sex, every moment you spend with them has to reinforce that free sexual desire in their minds and yours. All of your interactions with the beautiful women you want to fuck have to be about casual sex, and this has to happen from the very beginning.

This is a crown jewel in the game which flies right over the heads of men like aeroplanes, birds, and weed smoke. Why? Because the average American man believes he has to take women out on nice dates in order to fuck them. He and the women he wants to fuck have been socialised to believe this.

We can thank the mass media, popular culture, and deeply ingrained cultural traditions for teaching our fellow Americans to normalise this inappropriate behaviour. What far too many men fail to realise is that whenever they take women out to dinner and the movies or engage in activities which involve sitting, talking, eating, and drinking; women see they can enjoy the attention, money, and companionship they seek without having sex.

This is how women start to perceive men as potential boy-friends. This is how women manipulate and mould men into their future boyfriends and husbands instead of seeing them as men they can fuck with no strings attached. This is how men with little to no game with women lock themselves in the friend zone.

There's an indeterminable segment of the U.S. male population who approach women for hook ups and casual sex, but they take women out on dates and have the gall to complain when the women withhold casual sex. These men accuse the women of sending mixed signals and being attention whores and dick teasers, but they refuse to acknowledge the fact they were the first to send mixed signals after they approached women for casual sex and took them out on dates instead.

This is what happens when men who lack the courage to be straightforward with women say one thing, do another, and blame women for their failures to have casual sex. Please understand that the majority of the women you deal with are going to follow your lead. They're going to take their cues from the moves you make and the words you speak.

Therefore, if all you want from beautiful women is to have mind-blowing casual sex with them, don't take them out on dates. Dating is counter-productive to the true sexual desire in your heart. Be true to the game and be true to yourself. Don't take women out on dates if all you want to do is fuck them. I cannot stress this enough. Don't confuse these women or give them empty hopes and false expectations.

I'm going to break this down step-by-step because I don't want you to leave this chapter with any misunderstandings. This is where too many men with little to no experience with women shoot themselves in both feet and leave themselves lame in the game on bloody stumps.

Step 1: Let's assume you met this pretty woman named Betty Bubble Ass on Monday. She made your dick hard when you saw her. You approached her, told her you wanted to hook up with her on Friday night for a drink, and she agreed. You exchanged contact information and went your separate ways.

Step 2: Maintain zero contact from the time you met her on Monday until 7 p.m. on Thursday night, then send her one short text like this: What up, Betty? We still on for tmrw?

If she confirms the hook up for Friday, send this short text in return: Cool. TTYL.

That's it.

Don't call her because a phone call could open up a can of worms. She could flake on you and back out of the hook up, or you could say some goofy shit and talk yourself right out of the pussy. Follow these fun, easy steps from a man who knows who to get the pussy, and you can do the same.

Step 3: Meet Betty Bubble Ass at a bar within five to fifteen minutes walking distance from your home or the hotel/motel you're taking her to. Don't drink and drive and risk getting pulled over by the police.

Step 4: Let's assume Betty didn't flake on you, and she shows up at the bar on time. That's a win. Something about you made her want to see you again, which means you're in the arena. You can fuck this woman if you make the right seductive moves and speak the right seductive language.

Hug Betty when you greet her so you can initiate physical contact quickly. If she doesn't hug you, or if she gives you one of those stiff, don't pull me too close hugs, you already know she's not that comfortable with you. You already know the hook up might be an uphill battle. Sit somewhere cosy where you're close to each other and order the first round. If she offers to pay, tell her she can order the second round. Her buying you a drink might make up for that wack ass hug.

Don't waste time with a lot of small talk. Flirt with her physically and verbally, and get to the point. The best way to flirt with a woman is to be direct and get straight to the point. The only reason you want to hook up with Betty is because you want to fuck her and give her cum shots all over her face and tits, right? You have no interest in becoming her boyfriend or platonic friend. You just want to fuck the shit out of her, and the best way to make that happen is to talk about sex. Make eye contact with Betty and say this:

You: Can I tell you something?

Betty: Sure.

You: I asked you to meet me here because I think you're sexy. I don't want to be friends, and I don't want to get caught up in a serious relationship. I want to hook up for casual sex tonight, and for however long it lasts. No commitment. No strings. We just hook up and kick it.

What did you just do?

You just told Betty what you want from her in clean, direct, straightforward language within the first five minutes of the hook up. You got straight to the point. Good job. Now she has a choice to make. She will either decline your proposal and leave because she has low to no interest in having casual sex with you, or she'll stay because she wants to fuck and your direct approach just turned her on.

A certain amount of multitasking is required here. Touch Betty while you talk to her. One of the surest ways to gauge a woman's level of sexual interest in you is to touch her while you talk to her.

You already know you want to bend Betty over and bang the fuck out of her until you pass out. You knew this when you approached her. But you don't know if she has that same level of sexual interest in you, so you're going to gauge her sexual interest by flirting with her physically and verbally. If she allows you to do this and escalate, you're going to build the sexual tension until her pussy gets wet and she's ready to suck your dick and fuck the shit out of you.

When you say, "Betty, I think you're sexy," touch her hand. If she asks you not to touch her or if she moves her hand away, you know either she has low to no sexual interest in you, or there's someone else she's fucking. Whatever the case may be, if a woman gives you any resistance at this stage, pay for the drink(s) and cut the hook up shorter than Peter Dinklage.

If she doesn't move her hand away or ask you to stop touching her, that's your unspoken cue to continue. You're flirting with her to reinforce the message that this hook up is all about casual sex. You're flirting with her to build the sexual tension which is something the majority of the men she deals with fail to do, and you're communicating with her on two levels with body language and the spoken word. She might not listen to everything you say, but she feels your touch on her skin. Actions speak louder than words.

Step 5: If Betty doesn't stop you from touching her hand, move from her wrist up her arm. Test her boundaries and see if she's going to stop the physical escalation of your flirting. If she doesn't stop you, she's enjoying it. You're on the right track. When the drinks arrive, the alcohol will begin to work its chemical sex magic and don't think Betty doesn't realise what's going on. Don't be naive. Chances are this isn't her first rodeo. Women already know what the game is. They want to see if you know how to play.

If Betty doesn't stop you from touching her hand and arm, she likes how you're making her feel. Don't get nervous and stop. Touch her knee. If she doesn't object, leave your hand there for a moment and work your way up her thigh. Don't get super fucking thirsty and grab her by the pussy. You are not Donald Trump.

Step 6: If she hasn't stopped you from touching her at this point, you can safely assume she's feeling you and this fun, flirtatious space you've created. If she's shy, she might not be the first to reach out and touch you. If she's more aggressive, she might snuggle up to you and start touching you in return. You're building the sexual tension to the point where it explodes, and she kisses you.

You're building the sexual tension to encourage making out. Don't hesitate when you see your opportunity to kiss her. Don't get scared. Don't think twice. If she's willing to French kiss a man she just met off the street in a bar, there's lots of freaky shit you can and should do with this woman. Avoid being judgmental, and you can take full advantage of her true sexual nature.

There will be a moment in the conversation where talk lulls for a moment and your eyes meet hers. Stop talking when this happens. Don't look for something else to say. You've said enough. If you keep talking, you run the risk of saying some stupid ass shit, completely ruining the mood, and talking yourself right out of the pussy. You definitely don't want that to happen, so shut up and kiss her.

Step 7: Make out. Enjoy the moment. If she doesn't offer to suck your dick after five to ten minutes or so, tell her it's time to go. If she's feeling you and wants to fuck, she'll grab her purse, you'll pay the tab or split the bill if that's your arrangement, and you'll take her back to the crib, or your hotel/motel room.

This is a side-note, but it's also a caveat of the game too many men fail to consider. If Betty cooperates, you need to understand this hook up is an audition. Your game was strong enough to persuade her to give you an opportunity, so she wants to see if you can fuck her pussy the way she wants it to be fucked. There's pressure to perform well, and you need to know this going in.

If you fuck Betty well, turn her bubble ass out, and bring her to climax once or more, she might contact you to hook up again in future. She might not. There are no guarantees. If you fail to perform well, chances are you won't see or hear from her again. This is the nature of the sex game between men and women, and you need to be fully aware of this before you step into the arena.

The surest way to get Betty to come is from oral clitoral stimulation. The surest way to get Betty to come is to lick the pussy. The second-best way is to fuck her so well that you hit the bottom of the pussy. Use deep strokes along with deep French kisses to bring women to climax.

The key to controlling a woman is controlling her emotions. Women's emotional cores lie in their orgasms, and the key to controlling women is bringing them to sexual climax consistently. This is why it's essential to bring women to climax when you fuck them. Good dick is how you establish control. Good dick is how you establish dominance. There are three ways to fuck Betty (and other beautiful women you desire) and hit the bottom of the pussy. Pay attention.

Position 1: Doggy style. This is a classic. Leave Betty on her knees ass up on the bed for maximum depth and thrust. This position leaves one of your hands free, so use your fingers to stimulate her clitoris manually. You're welcome.

Position 2: The Rodeo: Lie down and allow Betty to mount you. Once she manuoeuvres into position, you should be good to go. Let Betty ease herself down on top of your dick and ride the shaft all the way down. If you're well-endowed, Betty (and practically every other woman you fuck) will thank God she finally met a cool dude with some good game and a big dick.

Position 3: The Buck. This goes all the way back to the 2 Live Crew. Put Betty in the missionary position, and push her legs as far back as they can go. This position leaves the pussy completely exposed, which makes it easier to hit the bottom and fuck her into submission.

Spend no more than one hour trying to persuade Betty (or any other woman you want to fuck) to go back to your crib or your hotel/motel room. If she's still not cooperating by then, pay the tab, tell her to have a good night, and be on your merry muthafucking way.

This is where the rubber meets the road. This is where you get to see what type of man you truly are. Full-dog alpha males, ladies' men, macks, players, and womanisers don't play games with deceptive women. Betty showed up at a bar to have drinks with a guy she just met off the street, which is you. She allowed you to touch her and kiss her in a public place, and when you invited her back to the crib, she said no? I know the game, so I know some bullshit when I hear it.

The truth is exactly what Betty isn't telling you, and the truth is she could be married. She could have a boyfriend. She could have a girlfriend. She could have a urinary tract infection. She could have herpes. She could've changed her mind. The truth is you don't know why Betty's not cooperating with you, and it's not your job to know why.

Fuck why she's not cooperating. You're in the game to have casual sex with the beautiful women you desire, and if women refuse to cooperate with you sexually, you have no time for them. At all. If Betty doesn't want to come back to your place, leave her in the bar and don't call or text her unless she calls or texts you first. If she never calls or texts you again, don't reach out to call or text her either. Charge her to the game and move on to more beautiful women.

Don't get weak and break down just because Betty has a dope body with a bubble ass. If you do, Betty (and the other women you deal with) will perceive you as another thirsty, weak-willed simp and play you accordingly. Having casual sex with multiple women isn't for every man, and there's nothing wrong if you realise this level of the game isn't for you.

Perhaps you don't want to fuck with multiple women. Perhaps you prefer to find one woman you can love as your long-term, monogamous girlfriend instead. Perhaps you're looking for your future wife. We all have different desires, needs, and wants, which is fine, but understand that you still need to master the game of getting women. You need to be just as well-versed in the game as the full-dog alpha males, ladies' men, macks, players, and womanisers even if you only want one woman to have, hold and fuck until death do you part.

I wrote this book to teach men how to play the game to their advantage, and fuck the beautiful women they desire. You can take women out on dates in attempts to romance them into bed, but that misguided approach may lead them to perceive you as boyfriend material. Or a sponsor, which is worse. The beautiful women you desire may not give you the pussy as quickly or as often as you would like, and it will be your own fault for going against the grain rather than humbling yourself before the wisdom of the game.

Let's give a quick recap as this chapter draws to a close. There's nothing wrong with wanting to fuck multiple women. Don't ever allow anyone to shame you because you want to fuck multiple women. You can have the casual sex you want with the beautiful women you desire, and you don't have to take them out on dates in order to fuck them.

Don't take women out on dates if all you want is casual sex from them. Meet them for drinks at a bar or lounge within five to fifteen minutes walking distance from your home or hotel/motel room. Spend no more than one hour at the bar or lounge flirting, touching and building sexual tension with these women. Kiss them, make out with them, and invite them to leave with you.

If women cooperate, take them back to your crib or hotel/motel room and fuck the shit out of them. Beat the pussy up like a convict fresh out of the penitentiary. Give these women a reason to hook up with you for casual sex in the future. If women don't cooperate, pay for the drink(s), tell them good night, and be on your merry muthafucking way. Leave them right there.

Don't stay and waste any more of your attention, money, and non-sexual time on uncooperative women. Don't call or text them unless they call or text you first. Move on and approach more beautiful women to have casual sex with. Don't give uncooperative women a second thought.

If you're approaching a minimum of one hundred new women per month for casual sex, you will have women who declined your invitation for casual sex at the bar or lounge call or text you at a later date to hang out. Don't hook up with any of these women at bars or lounges again. You tried that already.

Invite them over to your place to see if they're ready to fuck. Put them to the test. If they continue to play games like they don't want to have casual sex, tell them to leave. Put them out.

Don't ever allow women to sit in your crib and waste your time. I don't give a fuck how beautiful you think they are. Tell them to leave, charge them to the game, and delete their contact information from your mobile so you can't get weak, break down and reconnect with them later. You don't have to take women out on dates in order to fuck them. Be true to the game, and be true to yourself.

11 MAR 18 (SUN)
1724/The Valley
Mission Hills, Los Angeles, California

CHAPTER 5

Numbers Game

Have you ever heard sales is a numbers game?

If you work in sales, then you probably heard that your first day on the job. This is particularly true if you currently work or have ever worked as a telemarketer in a call centre.

Telemarketers learn sales is a numbers game from over-worked, under-appreciated floor managers who get paid to keep them on phones which ring non-stop with shitty leads. The average telemarketer takes hundreds of calls in one shift just to close a handful of deals.

I worked in a few call centres in LA. There's lots of phone work available in offices up and down Wilshire Boulevard in Koreatown, and two of my former jobs come to mind. I worked in a payday loan centre by MacArthur Park in the Westlake neighbourhood and a student loan forgiveness centre on Wilshire and Serrano.

I didn't enjoy telemarketing, but some days were better than others, I learned from the top sales reps around me, and I gradually became a closer. I learned how to seduce people over the phone and take their money, but I resented going to work because it took my time away from writing.

Writing is the love of my life. Writing is the chief priority in my life, but the cost of living in LA is exorbitant. This is a tough place to survive, but I'm still here by the grace of The

Most High doing my thing in the Entertainment Capital of the World. I was a top sales rep at the payday loan centre before I lost my job due to illness, and I found a job at the student loan forgiveness centre where I became the office manager.

I woke up way too goddamn early in the morning to shit, shower, shave, dress, eat breakfast, smoke weed, and take a crowded Red Line train to Koreatown where I answered hundreds of calls just to close a handfuls of deals for a rapacious business owner who didn't give two shits about me. Those who work in call centres can relate to this, but I digress…

I took hundreds of calls just to find five to ten decent leads I could close, and this is why sales is a numbers game. This is also why a lot of people don't like sales. They don't like people yelling at them, hurling obscenities, and hanging up the phone in their faces. They don't like rejection.

Hooking up with women for casual sex and taking them on dates is a numbers game too. This is where you have to decide what type of man you want to be. Do you really want to be a full-dog alpha male, ladies' man, mack, player, or womaniser with tight game who has casual sex with multiple women or not?

If you're serious about learning the game and having casual sex with multiple women, you have to approach a lot more women than you're normally used to. You're going to get rejected by the bulk of these women, and you need to know this going in.

Disreputable dating coaches and fraudulent pickup artists work to con you into believing you're not going to face serious rejection from women when you step into the arena. I'm not going to lie to you because there's no room for disingenuous bullshit in the game. Men who master the game identify who they truly are within and without. The first step to learning and mastering the game is being real with yourself at all times, and understanding what you truly want from women.

If you want to reinvent yourself as a man women find sexually attractive, you're going to approach the women you want to fuck, and the majority of them are going to reject you. They're going to shoot you down with M3 Browning anti-aircraft machine guns, so grow accustomed to hearing women tell you no. Prepare yourself for indifference, rejection, and time-wasting, attention-whoring foolishness if you're serious about this.

Full-dog alpha males, ladies' men, macks, players, and womanisers get rejected too. Everyone gets rejected. This is the nature of the game, but one of the crucial differences between you and them is that they know how to read women. They know how to read women quickly and correctly, they know which approach works best for them to get the pussy as soon as possible, so they aren't going to get rejected as often as you because they know how to maximise their sexual opportunities.

I share this with you because I don't want you to get discouraged. You're going to get rejected a lot at first because you lack confidence, experience, and skill. You're going to get rejected because you're not comfortable approaching the beautiful women you want to fuck. You're going to pretend you're comfortable, but you're not at ease, and the women you approach are going to see this. Women interpret your vibrations, so they're going to feel the insecurity and uncertainty in your energy despite your best efforts to mask them.

You're going to get rejected because you're unaccustomed to talking with beautiful women. The words aren't going to roll off of your tongue and flow naturally. You're going to be a bit awkward, and women are going to gun you down with the big Brownings. However, if you dedicate yourself and open your mind to practising and mastering the game of getting women, and if you approach the beautiful women you want to fuck every day and remain consistent despite the constant barrage of rejection, you're going to start learning the game.

You're going to develop confidence in yourself. You're going to develop skill and wit in the game of seduction because you're going to learn what works and what doesn't work for you. You're going to learn what you should and shouldn't say. You're going to learn that less said is best said. You're going to learn how to get women sexually aroused with your words, and you're not going to get rejected as often.

More beautiful women are going to choose you, they're going to show up for hook ups and dates with you, they're going to have casual sex with you, suck your dick and swallow your seed. The rejection never stops completely. Make your peace with that reality right now. Don't let any of these crooked ass dating coaches and underhanded pickup artists piss in your face, call it rain, and run off with your money. There are popular male celebrities who get rejected by women.

You might be surprised by this. You shouldn't be. Celebrities have fame, social status, and wealth, and those are enviable attributes coveted all over the world, but they don't give men authentic sex appeal and tight game with women. Fame, social status, and wealth don't stop men from being simps, sponsors, or weak muthafuckas with women in general. Fame, social status, and wealth aren't guaranteed to get women's vaginas wet, and male celebrities with little to no game find this out the hard way.

Women love having casual sex with men who get their pussies wet, and a celebrity might not be one of those guys. Some famous men with fragile egos refuse to understand and accept this rather unpleasant reality, so their arrogance and bruised egos drive them to indulge in domestic abuse, rape and sexual assault which is foolish, needless, pathetic, and weak.

All men suffer rejection from the women they want to fuck at some point in their lives, but the full-dog alpha males, ladies' men, macks, players, and womanisers overcome those rejections where others fail, and they fuck the beautiful women they desire without paying them for sexual favours, promising monogamy, or spending non-sexual companionship with them.

Hooking up with beautiful women for casual sex is a numbers game. Approaching beautiful women for dates is a numbers game too. You're going to get rejected, you already know this going in, so don't get scared. If you don't approach the beautiful women you desire and get rejected from those who don't like you, you're never going to meet the beautiful women who actually like you and want to have casual sex with you.

If you're reading these words and don't believe this can happen for you, you're in the right place at the right time reading the right book for something amazing to happen in your life. You lack confidence in yourself, but I'm going to help you with that deficiency. Help me to help you.

You can put yourself where you want to be in terms of having casual sex with the beautiful women you desire, but you won't accomplish this without drinking deeply from the bitter chalice of rejection. Many times. It's not cool, it's not fair, we all fucking hate that shit when it happens, but it is what it is.

4 MAR 18 (SUN)
0537/Starbucks Coffee
on Lankershim and Magnolia
North Hollywood, Los Angeles, California

CHAPTER 6

Confidence Game

A confidence game is defined as an attempt to defraud a person or group after gaining their confidence and trust. The perpetrator of a confidence game is often referred to as a confidence man, con man, or con artist. A thriving confidence man peddles in charm and deceit and swindles gullible men, women and unwary businesses out of their money and other assets. Craftiness, fraud, and magnetism are the tools of his trade, and he runs the flimflam on people successfully because he's able to persuade them he can be relied upon.

If you want to hook up with and date multiple women, you're going to become a confidence man of sorts, but you're not going to defraud them out of the pussy. I don't advocate deceit, and when you're well-versed in the game, there's no need for you to resort to dishonesty, duplicity, treachery, trickery or any other type of underhanded behaviour.

Full-dog alpha males, ladies' men, macks, players, and womanisers don't lie and defraud women out of the pussy. These men have casual sex with multiple women, the women they fuck know this, and everyone involved accepts the game as it is. It's this acceptance from their lovers, the power of honesty, and their indomitable confidence, which gives those men the carnal vibes and sexual energy women find irresistible.

These men are honest about who they are, what they're about, and what they want from women. Honesty is transparent, and it creates confidence and happiness within. Deceit is opaque, it creates guilt and shame within, and there's no reason to take that route. Not when you can learn the game of having sex with multiple beautiful women and develop the confidence which lies within you.

What is confidence? The belief in oneself and one's powers or abilities. Confidence is self-reliance. Self-assurance. Confidence and a healthy heaping of lust push you to approach the beautiful women you want to fuck. Confidence is an aphrodisiac which compels women to cooperate with you sexually.

Confidence is the backbone of the game, and I cannot stress this enough. Confidence is the essence and foundation of the game, and it flies directly in the faces of those who claim all men need are looks, money, and status in order to have casual sex with beautiful women. There's an ongoing debate within the dating community online and offline as to which men enjoy the most sexual success with beautiful women.

One group claims the men with the best looks, the most money, and the highest social statuses enjoy the most casual sex with beautiful women. We'll call these guys the Looks, Money, and Status Camp.

The opposing group claims full-dog alpha males, ladies' men, macks, players, and womanisers; the men who use charm, confidence, personality, and raw sex appeal are the men who seduce and enjoy the most casual sex with beautiful women. These men belong to the Game School. These camps go back and forth, and it can be entertaining at times, but I see no debate here for three reasons:

- First, a man's looks don't seduce a woman.

    This may come as a slap in the face to some of you, especially if you're in the Looks, Money, and Status

Camp. The truth often has a demoralising effect on delusional people, and one of the purposes of this book is to identify and crush comfortable falsehoods, misconceptions, and stereotypes reinforced by defective American social programming and human ignorance.

What I find interesting and a bit odd is how men in the Looks, Money, and Status Camp tend to base their looks argument on how handsome a man's face is as opposed to a man's physique and overall appearance. There's nothing wrong with having a handsome face. All bullshit aside, I don't know a single man who would prefer not to be handsome and chances are you don't either.

What these men fail to realise, however, is that there are plenty of handsome guys who still struggle to attract and fuck the women they desire. Women have no probably telling these men they're handsome, but they're not having sex with them. Just because a woman finds you attractive doesn't mean she will get butt ass naked, suck your dick, let you fuck her in every hole, and swallow your seed with a smile.

The ugly truth the men in the Looks, Money, and Status Camp refuse to accept is that women want to have casual sex with men who give them sexual sparks and make their pussies wet. A handsome face doesn't get a woman's pussy wet. If you're a man concerned about your looks and you want to find the best way to attract the women you desire, then take your overall appearance into account.

Stop obsessing over your face which isn't getting you any pussy, and work on your body. Trim the fat, get lean, and develop rock hard muscles. Women don't fuck your face. Women fuck your body, and they prefer to feel chiselled, rock hard muscles on top of them. Remember this the next time people start talking about looks. Take some boxing classes too. The sweet science helps you develop confidence, a ripped physique, and you'll learn how to defend yourself without a firearm. You're welcome.

- Second, a man's money and status aren't guaranteed to get a woman's pussy wet.

If that sounds completely ridiculous to some of you, I'm sure you fall into that indeterminable percentage of men who struggle to attract and fuck beautiful women.

There's nothing wrong with having money and high social status. Perhaps you received wealth and status by virtue of your birth and family name. Perhaps you had to work for it where your endeavours and innate talents brought fame and wealth to you. Enjoy whatever you've been blessed with, but don't think your money and status are going to generate insatiable sexual attraction in the women you desire if you haven't done anything to arouse them yourself.

Full-dog alpha males, ladies' men, macks, players, and womanisers use charisma, charm, personality, seductive language, and game they've learned from their ample sexual experiences. They flirt with women and maintain unwavering eye contact to draw them in. They touch women while they flirt and build sexual tension every step of the way. They do what it takes to get women sexually aroused instead of depending on their money and status to do the heavy lifting for them.

We examined the true sexual nature of women and determined it's not in their nature to be monogamous. There isn't any empirical evidence to prove women are biologically hard-wired to be monogamous. There isn't any empirical evidence to prove women don't get bored with monogamy just like men do. Men forced monogamy upon women for millennia, but women's true sexual nature is given to deception because human nature is deceitful for the most part, so women are just as capable of being dishonest, lying scumbags as men are.

Women are just as sexually deceptive as men are and I have no problem acknowledging this because I've found it to be true. Especially if we're talking about women born in the U.S. after 1960.

I'm neither frightened nor threatened by the true sexual nature of women, but there are multitudes of men who refuse to understand and accept this simple truth. Deep down, these men cannot accept the fact women are just as deceptive as they are, so they choose to lie to themselves and convince themselves women are naturally more monogamous than men somehow.

This is a lie these delusional men have grown comfortable telling themselves and others. This is a lie which makes these men feel safe and secure. This is a lie which helps these men sleep better at night and roll out of their beds to face their lives the next day. The men who tell themselves all they need are money and status to attract and have casual sex with beautiful women are lying to themselves as well. Don't be fooled into believing a man's money and status are guaranteed to arouse women sexually and get their pussies wet.

- Third, confidence arouses women sexually on emotional and physical levels.

There's something alluring about a man who approaches the women he wants to fuck and communicates his sexual desire with confidence and a direct, seductive approach. Women will reject him occasionally, but they won't forget the boldness with which he approached them and damn near seduced them before they finally scraped up enough resistance to say no.

The word no came out of their mouths even as their pussies said yes. The pussy can say yes even as a woman objects because the bold man's confidence stirs something ravenous between her thighs. Women don't forget the men who give them those deep carnal vibrations.

Why are women attracted to confident men?

Confidence is an aphrodisiac and a source of comfort. Women feel confident men will be able to take care of them regardless of what happens. Too many men refuse to realise and accept this, but confidence is a stimulant which intoxicates women like a double shot of Hennessy cognac with no chaser, and this intoxication turns into sexual attraction.

I would be remiss if I failed to acknowledge the women who target and stalk men with money and status specifically. These women are known more commonly as gold diggers. The term gold digger carries negative connotations and elicits harsh judgment and sharp indignation from many, but I don't criticise gold diggers or the men who choose to sponsor them.

Gold diggers are players in the social phenomenon we call the game, and if those women are successful in locating, charming, seducing, and ultimately exploiting men with money and status who are gullible enough to swallow their bullshit hook, line, and sinker and return for additional helpings, I won't criticise gold diggers for achieving their objectives. How can I criticise them for winning?

I don't criticise the men with money and status who sponsor gold diggers because they're receiving exactly what they're paying for. People don't appear to understand that gold digging is a transactional relationship where the people involved willingly engage in romance for money rather than love.

The key word here is willingly. A gold digger is willing to enjoy all of a man's money, status and non-sexual companionship she possibly can in exchange for providing the minimum of sexual attention and companionship required to maintain her transactional relationship.

The beta male; also known as an easy mark, simp, trick or man with money and status in this example knows he's involved in a transactional relationship, and he's willing to finance this arrangement in exchange for sexual attention and companionship the gold digger gives him. A transactional relationship is a business with benefits and an unspoken contract where both parties cooperate willingly with each other. Both parties are in agreement.

Men with confidence and game have casual sex with beautiful women. Men with looks, money and status do the same. The key difference, however, is men with confidence and game don't need looks, money, and status to fuck beautiful women and have casual relations. The game levels the playing field in one of the most critical areas of human activity, which is sex.

There's nothing wrong with having looks, money, and status. Virtually every American male I know would love to have beauty, fame, and wealth in abundance, but this is where I have to separate the game from the truth. A woman may appreciate a man's looks and covet his money and status, but she will lust after and have casual sex with the man who has enough confidence and game to approach her, look her directly in her eyes, and tell her exactly what he wants to do to her.

Confidence is the backbone of the game, and I cannot stress this enough. You might lack confidence in yourself right now, and that's okay. I did too at one point, but I developed and strengthened my game and confidence like muscles. This is why it's also referred to as self-confidence or self-assurance.

Full-dog alpha males, ladies' men, macks, players, and womanisers receive harsh criticism from other men and women alike. Some of the criticism is warranted no doubt, but an indeterminable percentage of it is steeped in envy and resentment of their unwavering confidence in themselves. Some people hate the very sight of a man with a firm belief in himself, and unconfident men tend to be the worst when it comes to this.

If confidence was a tradable financial asset on the stock market, more men would have hallowed respect for it. Confidence, however, is intangible. It's a masterful attribute which flows from deep within one's spirit.

Many men fail to build confidence in themselves despite their best efforts, and they become scornful in their defeat. They develop bitter envy and hatred for the men who shine in the light of their self-assurance and condemn confidence as worthless when nothing could be further from the truth.

As this chapter draws to a close, I must reiterate that confidence and emotional connections turn women on sexually. Not your looks, money, and status. If you want to have casual sex with multiple women, you have to connect with them emotionally. They aren't going to make real emotional connections with your looks, money, or status, and if you depend on those ornaments to make those vital connections for you, you're going to be frustrated. I won't apologise for bursting your bubble.

A woman makes a real emotional connection with a confident man because she's attracted to his self-assurance. His undeniable belief in himself pulls her to him like a magnet, his game draws her in, and his flirting and seductive talk gets her sexually aroused. Reinvent yourself as a confidence man. This will change how you dress, talk, and walk. This will change how you think about women and yourself, so be confident in all of your dealings with beautiful women from the moment you meet them.

10 MAR 18 (SAT)
0534/The Valley
Mission Hills, Los Angeles, California

CHAPTER 7

Approach Women And Get To The Point/Assume The Pussy

I'm going to ask you a few questions, and I want you to be honest with yourself. To thine own self be true as Shakespeare wrote in *Hamlet*. How many times have you seen a beautiful woman you wanted to fuck so bad your dick got hard, but you didn't approach her, she walked right on by, and you never saw her again? How many times have you allowed this to happen?

Don't lie to me and don't lie to yourself. To thine own self be true.

Is that a tough question to answer? Good. Here's another one. Why didn't you approach her? Your dick got hard as an Angolan diamond when you saw her. You wanted to fuck her with all of the strength in your body. Why didn't you tell her that? The answer is simple. You got scared.

Your fear of rejection from a beautiful woman you wanted to fuck outweighed your desire to approach her and have casual sex. You're accustomed to fearing rejection from women, so you denied yourself the opportunity to approach her for casual sex which she might have agreed to, and you couldn't stop staring at her bubble ass as she walked away.

Does this sound about right? I thought so. Here's another uncomfortable question for you to ponder. Why are you so afraid to approach beautiful women for casual sex? I ask this because I want you to understand your fear of rejection from beautiful women isn't the root of your problem. It's a symptom to be sure, but it's not the root cause.

You choose not to approach the beautiful women you want to fuck because you've already decided beautiful women don't like you, and they don't want to have casual sex with you. Please bear in mind these women never turned you down because you never spoke to them. You never flirted with them. You never gave them the opportunity to accept you or reject you.

You made that decision for them. You took yourself out of the game without running a single play, and you did so for two reasons. One, you lack the confidence to approach the comely women you desire for casual sex. You have little to no confidence in yourself, and women intimidate you. Two, you have low to no self-esteem. You don't like yourself. In fact, you dislike yourself so much you can't see why comely women would be attracted to you at all.

You're the problem in these situations. You're the one with little to no confidence in yourself and low to no self-esteem. Those are your shortcomings. You can blame women for your frailties as weak men are wont to do, but that pathetic deflection and denial won't make you any stronger in the game. At all.

You can be cross with beautiful women for not approaching you because you're too afraid to initiate conversation and chat them up yourself, but that cowardly, evasive cop-out won't give you the confidence and courage to approach beautiful women and make the first move. At all.

Your fear, lack of confidence, and low self-esteem erect invisible barricades between you and the beautiful women you desire. These hindrances will block your progress and retard your growth in the game until you clear them by approaching the comely women you want to fuck, looking them in their eyes, and telling them you want to hook up with them for casual sex or take them out on dates. This requires a full grown set of balls and firm backbone because you're leaving yourself wide open to rejection.

This might not sound like a big deal to the uninitiated, but approaching women for casual sex is no small feat. In fact, there's an indeterminable segment of the world's male population who lack the balls and backbone to approach the beautiful women they want to fuck, look them in their eyes, and tell them what their true intentions are. There's nothing easy about any of this, but it's the best way to break the plane of fear you've created for yourself. You have to put yourself out there to be accepted or rejected by women sexually. You have to assume the pussy.

When you fail to assume the pussy doubt and fear enter your mind. Doubt inspires you to pause. Doubt makes you think twice instead of following your first mind and taking action. Fear freezes you in your tracks like an inexperienced soldier under enemy fire for the first time who's scared shitless and unable to squeeze the trigger even though he has the enemy locked in the sights of his weapon.

One of the reasons you get scared is because you don't know what to say to women to get your point across. Don't trip, homie. I'm here to help you in the areas where you struggle most, so the next time you see a beautiful woman who gets your dick harder than a double life sentence you aren't going to surrender to your doubt and fear. You aren't going to let her just walk right out of your life like you have so many times before.

You're going to approach her instead. You're going to make eye contact and get to the point even though you're scared, your words are stuck in your throat, and you're uncomfortable as shit because this is new, uncharted territory for you. I'm going to give you two options on how to approach beautiful women and assume the pussy. Choose the option which suits you best.

Option #1 - Approach the beautiful woman you want to fuck and make eye contact.

You: Hi. What's your name?

(Wait for her to tell you her name.)

You: My name is _____, and I think you're sexy. We need to hook up this weekend. Put my number in your phone. (If she's interested in you sexually, she'll cooperate willingly.) Call/text me (give her a specific day and time to call/text you), so we can hook up and kick it. It was nice meeting you. Talk to you later.

That's it. See how simple this is? You should be in and out of this woman's face in forty-five seconds to two minutes tops. You can muster enough confidence and courage to do this. If you can't, you might want to leave the game of getting women alone. This might not be for you.

Option #1 is for novices. This option allows for those with little to no self-esteem and confidence in themselves to approach the women they desire with a straightforward verbal approach. The best way to improve your confidence and self-esteem is to approach the beautiful women you want to have casual sex with.

Perhaps you feel intimidated when you see beautiful women. Maybe you think they're too pretty for you to approach them. The fear you feel tightening around your balls is natural and you're going to walk right through it. You're going to approach that woman, introduce yourself, and get to the point.

Tell her you want to hook up for casual sex, or you want to date her. Some of these women are going to reject you, and kick you straight to the curb without any hesitation. Some of them are going to fuck your fucking brains out. You win some, and you lose some. This is the nature of the game. No one wins them all. Don't believe the hype.

If she doesn't cooperate, then it's your call if you want to continue. You may want to go back and forth with her as to why she should take your number, but experience has taught me not to linger on women who are uncooperative.

If women are uncooperative when you first meet them, and you pursue them anyway, you're giving them far too much leeway, and they will feel comfortable giving you resistance in future. Don't grovel at the feet of any of these women. Ever. Leave them alone and move on.

Conversely, if the beautiful woman cooperates, that's a victory for you. She liked what she saw, and she wants to see more. You're not guaranteed to fuck her because she put your contact info in her mobile, but it's a step in the process. You're putting yourself in position to get the pussy, and it's a good sign when beautiful women cooperate straight from the gate.

- This is pure game, and I don't want you to miss this jewel. Don't ask beautiful women to put your contact information in their mobiles. Use assumptive language and tell them to do it. Assume they're going to take your contact information.
- People rarely do what you ask them to do. If you ask someone to do something, they will refuse and tell you no more often than not. This is a natural instinct for an indeterminable segment of the human population which certainly appears to be the majority.
- People don't do what you ask them to do. People do what you *tell* them to do. This is simply how people are wired. Don't ask beautiful women to do anything for you. Tell them how they're going to serve you in assumptive language. Give them specific instructions. Establish yourself as the person in control from your first encounter with them, and remain consistent in that role. Put the game to work for you.

My readers who work in sales or have prior work experience in sales are familiar with the concept and practise of assuming the close. For those unfamiliar with the term, assuming the close means a sales professional assumes the client/customer/prospect is going to purchase the product or service being sold. A seasoned sales professional uses a deft, subtle touch to let the client/customer/prospect know it's assumed he/she is going to make the purchase.

This is a highly effective, persuasive closing tactic in sales, and it translates directly to sex and the game of seduction. Assume the comely women you desire are going to fuck you when you flirt with them. Assume they're going to ride the dick like a rodeo. Assume the pussy the same way real estate agents assume the close when they show properties to potential homeowners with good to excellent credit and money to spend.

Option #2 is for bold men. It's sexually explicit, which works best for men who aren't shy about stating their true intentions through straightforward language.

Option #2 - Approach the beautiful woman and make eye contact.

You: Hi. What's your name?

(Wait for her to tell you her name.)

You: My name is _____. It's nice to meet you. Listen, I saw you over here looking good, and you got my dick harder than prison time. We need to hook up. I'm free to make you come this weekend. Put my number in your phone. (If she's interested, she'll follow directions.) Call/text me (give her a specific day and time to call/text you), so I can get you butt ass naked and put my dick down your throat. Talk to you later.

That's it. Pitch her in forty-five seconds to two minutes tops. Option #2 is direct like a laser beam. You're assuming the pussy from hello, and Option #2 can lead to an indeterminable percentage of women fucking you ten to twenty minutes after first meeting them if you pitch them with the right confidence and delivery.

Some women will take offence because your approach was just too curt, too direct, and too erotic for their tastes. Some of them will brush you off, yell at you, or curse you out and make a scene. Don't trip. Smile and take it in stride.

Don't become cross with them. Your hardcore approach caught them off-guard and rubbed them the wrong way, but they heard what you said. Your words hit home, and if they're attracted to you sexually, you'll end up fucking some of these women days, weeks, or maybe a month or two later.

It's beautiful when this happens because you already stated your position clearly; you laid your game down quite flat, these women already know where you stand, and they're ready and willing to play your game.

Option #2 helps you talk your way into casual sex with the beautiful women you want to fuck because you bypass phoney, tedious, small talk and other false pleasantries to get straight to the point. You're taking a direct approach which gives women the sexual freedom to respond in kind if they're interested. Approach the women you want to have casual sex with, introduce yourself, and get straight to the point. Assume the pussy.

Wear condoms when you bang these women out. You want hot, toe-curling, casual sex with no strings attached. I know how good it feels to run up in the pussy raw balls deep. There's nothing quite like that sensation, however, you don't want to contract sexually transmitted diseases or make unwanted children with women you don't love and want to spend the rest of your life with.

13 MAR 18 (TUES)
2314/West Hollywood, Los Angeles, California
Skybar at Mondrian

CHAPTER 8

Maintain Zero Contact/Confirm The Date

You were grocery shopping on Monday night when you saw a beautiful woman you wanted to fuck. You already know how I feel about the one to ten ranking system of sexual attraction, but for the sake of argument, let's assume this woman was a nine in terms of her physical appearance.

You worked up the nerve to approach her, and you didn't stumble over your words. You told her you wanted to hook up with her on Friday night and have a drink. She smiled, said okay, and you exchanged contact information.

You gave her instructions to call you at eight p.m. sharp Thursday night. She agreed, and you two went your separate ways. If you're doing the Game 100 Challenge, this is the type of woman you want to meet when you're out prowling for pussy.

Now it's Tuesday afternoon, and you're bored at the crib thinking about how you met Miss Hot Girl at the grocery store. You keep thinking about how sexy she looked. You keep thinking about how bad you want to bend her over. You can't wait to see her again, so you grab your mobile to send her a text.

Stop.

You're simping already, and you just met this woman.

Stop simping and put your mobile down.

Now.

You haven't touched her, kissed her or fucked her yet, but you're already putting her up on a pedestal.

You're fucking up.

Stop simping and put your mobile down.

Now.

This is how guys with little to no experience with women and little to no game shoot themselves in both feet with double-barrelled Mossberg shotguns and leave themselves lame in the game on bloody stumps. You told Miss Hot Girl to call you at eight p.m. sharp on Thursday night, right? That means maintain zero contact with her until then. Don't call or text her any sooner because she could flake on you.

Calling her also increases the chances of you talking too much and saying something stupid which could ruin the hook up or date before it has a chance to happen. A phone call is unnecessary, and it could quite possibly undermine your sexual objective.

You want to see if she's able to follow directions and call you when you told her to. If she follows directions, you don't need to send her a text. However, let's assume it's nine p.m. on Thursday night, and you still haven't heard from Miss Hot Girl. She hasn't followed your directions, so send one short text to confirm the hook up or date. Your text should read: What's up? We still on for tmrw?

That's it. No more, no less.

If she confirms, send another short text: Cool. TTYL.

That's it. No more, no less.

Resume zero contact from that point (meaning no calls, emails, text messages, or any other type of communication) until you meet her for the hook up or date.

You think you like Miss Hot Girl, and that's a big part of your problem. You like her too goddamn much, and you just met her. You don't even know this woman.

So you think she's beautiful. So the fuck what? Never let the physical comeliness of women blind you, homie. Don't call or text women you want to have casual sex with during zero contact for two reasons.

First, when a woman meets a man she likes, she starts fantasising about him. She starts building images in her mind about what type of man he might be, so the last thing you want to do is interrupt her fantasy with your simpleton reality. You met her on Monday, so let her mind wander and dwell on you until eight p.m. Thursday night.

If she really likes you, her wonderment will become sexual interest and willingness to hook up with you or show up for the date on Friday night. She wants to see if you're going to measure up to or exceed the mental image she's already created in her mind. She also wants to see how well you perform sexually.

The average man becomes so thirsty for a woman's intimacy and the possibility of casual sex that he underestimates the power of suspense. Miss Hot Girl might harbour her own insecurities you're completely unaware of. You think she's a nine, but that's your opinion. Beauty is in the eye of the beholder. She might see herself as a seven. Or a six.

She might think you're the best looking guy she's met in months, and she's not sure whether you like her or not. She's not sure where she stands with you, and this is exactly where you want her to be.

You want to keep her suspended in incertitude and use her insecurities to your advantage. Men who are skilled and well-schooled in the game already know they have to keep women off balance emotionally. This is because women don't get super excited to have casual sex with the men who validate them.

An indeterminable percentage of women disregard, ignore and pass over the men who love them because devoted men don't present any sort of sexual challenge to them. There are always exceptions, but this tends to hold true for the most part.

You may or may not be aware of this, but there's an indeterminable segment of female teens and adult women around the world who crave challenges and love chasing guys who aren't all that into them. Miss Hot Girl agreed to see you, so allow her to wonder about you and work that shit to your advantage. Don't disturb her fantasy with your needy, simpish insecurity. Maintain zero contact and allow the suspense to build.

Second, if you break zero contact, and call or text Miss Hot Girl, you're going to look clingy in her eyes. You're going to look needy. You're going to look like a jelly back simp who doesn't get women and even if that's who you are right now you should be working to change that ASAFP. You should be reinventing yourself into a bold, confident, decisive, self-assured man beautiful women want to have casual sex with.

At the end of the day, you want to be the man beautiful women want to suck and fuck, and he doesn't meet a woman on Monday night and call or text her Tuesday afternoon. He uses suspense to his advantage by letting it build. He sends one text the night before the hook up or date to confirm because he understands the significance of keeping Miss Hot Girl on the edge of her seat emotionally to increase his chances of fucking her brains out.

He understands the importance of cultivating an air of mystery to attract beautiful women. He understands mystery is an irresistible aphrodisiac more powerful than money. Keep Miss Hot Girl guessing. The game will work out in your favour. Let her wonder about what you're going to wear, whether or not she looks fat in her favourite jeans, and how you're going to kiss her.

Practise some discipline, restrain your simpish instincts, and maintain zero contact until Thursday night at eight p.m. to confirm the hook up or date. Let the game work for you. This is part of how you reinvent yourself and make yourself more attractive to the beautiful women you desire. If Miss Hot Girl doesn't text you back to confirm the hook up or date, you will maintain zero contact permanently. She wasn't feeling you, and that's cool.

You might be pissed as shit, but it's all good, homie. Accept it as such. Women don't have to hook up with you, nor do they have to go out on dates with you. Maybe no one ever took the time to tell you how the world really works, so this may come as a bit of a shock, but women don't owe you sex or companionship.

Truthfully speaking, women don't owe you jack shit, and you don't owe them jack shit either. If you're campaigning for the pussy like a true player, you understand this concept, and you're approaching the women you want to fuck every day. An indeterminable percentage of them are going to reject you, but if your game is tight, some of them are going to cooperate with you and take dick in every hole.

I know this to be true from personal experience, and you're never going to taste that kind of sexual satisfaction by simping. Calling and texting too much turns women off which is the complete opposite of what you're trying to accomplish, so don't do that goofy shit.

Let's have a quick recap. When you approach women for hook ups or dates, give them clear instructions on what day and time you want them to contact you. Maintain zero contact until the night before you're supposed to hook up or go out on the date. If the woman fails to follow instructions and contact you by the time agreed upon, send one short text to confirm. The text should go something like this. What's up? We still on for tmrw?

That's it. No more, no less.

If she texts you back, you reply, Cool. TTYL.

That's it. No more, no less.

Maintain zero contact. And stop thinking about Miss Hot Girl so goddamn much. Put her out of your mind until it's time to confirm the hook up or date, and go approach more beautiful women you want to have casual sex with. Don't allow yourself to get weak for any of these women. Ever. Fuck how beautiful you think they are. The Most High never made a woman who looks nearly as good as one million dollars in cash, so stand strong in the game and maintain zero contact.

2 MAR 18 (FRI)
1737/Kokio Chicken
Koreatown, Los Angeles, California

CHAPTER 9

A Word About Flaking

Rejection is an inevitable, unavoidable part of the game when you're dealing with women. No man is safe from rejection, and no man is spared. You can be an ice-cold, full-dog alpha male, ladies' man, mack, player, or womaniser with next level game tighter than fish pussy, and you'll still meet women who will reject you.

You can be a man blessed with movie star good looks, money, and high social status, and you'll still meet women who will reject you too. No man is safe from rejection, and no man is spared.

Men don't appreciate being rejected by women. An indeterminable segment of the world's male population grows violent in their words and deeds when they find themselves rebuffed by the women they want to have sex with. This is how men catch rape and sexual assault felony charges and get locked up in the bowels of the prison-industrial complex. This is something men can avoid altogether.

You don't have to fall into this trap, saddle yourself with a criminal record, and fuck your life up if you understand and accept the fact that rejection is an inevitable, unavoidable part of the game if you want to have casual sex with multiple women. Take rejection in stride when it happens, and keep campaigning for casual sex with more beautiful women.

What is flaking? Flaking is a slang term which means to renege on a social engagement. A woman flakes on you when she agrees to meet you for a hook up or a date and then decides not to show up.

Have you ever gotten a woman's contact information, set up a hook up or date, and she never showed up at the bar, lounge, movie theatre, restaurant, or wherever you were supposed to meet her? She flaked on you.

Have you ever invited a woman over to your place or a hotel/motel room for a fuck session and she agreed to come by, but then she never showed up? She flaked on you. No man is safe from flaking, and no man is spared. Here are three points I want you to take away from this chapter.

1. Don't take flaking personally. Flaking is an inevitable, unavoidable part of the game as I've already pointed out. It's not a question of if women are going to flake on you. It's a question of when they're going to flake on you, and once you take flaking personally, you run the risk of getting annoyed, angry, and frustrated with the women who flaked on you as well as yourself.

Don't give those negative emotions free rein because they can take funny twists and turns. Your unchecked annoyance, anger, and frustration can turn into uncertainty where you begin to doubt yourself, and those nagging inner doubts can throw you off your game.

If you remain focused on the women who flake on you and allow your doubt and insecurity to take root, you will grow timid and unsure when you see the beautiful women you want to fuck. Your fear, doubt, and insecurity will gnaw away at you, and you won't take action when it's time for you to be confident and step to beautiful women with no hesitation.

All of this is counterproductive to what you're trying to accomplish in the game. You're building your confidence. You're building your self-esteem. You're becoming your best self, so don't put yourself through unnecessary emotional foolishness.

Don't take flaking personally. When women flake on you, brush their rejection off, take it in stride, and keep campaigning to fuck the beautiful women you desire. Don't ever allow a flake to shake your confidence.

2. Don't dwell on the women who flake on you. When women flake on you, don't waste your time wondering why. I've seen far too many men waste time, and get bogged down trying to deconstruct why women flaked on them and didn't show up for hook ups and dates.

Let's break this down with what used to be known as common sense. Does it really matter why a woman flaked on you? Does pondering the unknown reason(s) why a woman flaked on you actually bring you any closer to fucking her? No, it doesn't.

She might've flaked on you because she had to hang out with her husband. There's an indeterminable segment of the world's sexually active female population who won't tell you they're married. She might've flaked on you because she has a boyfriend. Or a girlfriend. She might've flaked on you because one of her friends invited her to a concert. Or a club. Or a party. And she forgot about you in half a second.

She could've gotten into a serious car accident on her way over to your place to suck your dick and swallow the cum. Or, the man she really wanted to suck and fuck texted her, told her to be butt ass naked on her knees when he walks through the door, and she forgot about you instantly.

Dwelling on why women flake on you doesn't bring you any closer to having casual sex with them. It's a waste of time much better spent approaching and flirting with more beautiful women you want to hook up with or date.

Dwelling on why women flaked on you doesn't change the fact they reneged on your social engagement, and your emotional fixation on the negative will rattle and undermine the confidence and self-esteem you're trying to build and reinforce within yourself.

And if you aren't having casual sex with the beautiful women you desire on a regular basis, your confidence and self-esteem aren't where they need to be. You have a lot of self-improving to do, you don't need to waste time, and you don't need to entertain negative energy and self-destructive thoughts which will only discourage you. Nine times out of ten, the women who flake on you won't show up for hook ups or dates because they don't see you as a high-priority man.

The women who flake on you place little to no value on you, your time, and your companionship. To be perfectly curt, you don't mean shit to these women, so why should you waste half a second of your life pondering why they flaked on you? Do you honestly think any of those women are thinking about you while they're fucking and sucking the dicks of the men they desire most?

3. Don't call or text the women who flake on you because this makes you look clingy, needy, and weak. When you're not well-versed in the game and have little to no experience with women, you don't know how to deal with flakes most effectively. You fail to understand how and why you should starve rude flakes by withholding your attention, non-sexual companionship, and time the way ruthless warlords withhold food and water and starve seditious rebels into submission. When you're not well-versed in the game and have little to no experience with women, you fail to understand they're more addicted to attention than dick and money.

This critical fact goes right over your head like birds and police helicopters, so when women flake on you, it's your first instinct to call and text them to see what happened. That's an inappropriate response when women flake on you. Especially if they lacked the decency to call or text, and tell you they couldn't make the hook up or date.

Flaking is an inevitable, unavoidable element of the game. No man is safe from flaking, and no man is spared. Don't take exception when it happens to you. When women flake on you instead of showing up for hook ups and dates don't call or text them to see if they're okay. Fuck if they're okay.

That's not your concern. Don't call or text them to find out what happened. Fuck what happened. There are consequences for the dimwits who violate the rules of the game, and if you call or text women who flake on you, you're going to look like a clingy, needy, weak-minded, jelly back simp which might be what you really are underneath it all.

When a woman flakes on you, and you call or text her to check up on her, she knows she has you in the palm of her hand. She hasn't had sex with you. She's probably never going to have sex with you, but you're ready and willing to give yourself to her anyway. She knows you're absolutely no challenge at all, and you fail to understand how unsexy and weak this makes you in her eyes.

You also fail to understand that she flaked on you to go fuck and suck the dick of the man (or men) she really wants. Then you call and text her to find out what happened and see how she's doing? Does that make any sense at all?

No, it doesn't. That simp ass shit sounds weak as fuck, and it makes you look weak as fuck too. You're giving her your attention, non-sexual companionship, and time (which women covet) after she flaked on you.

You're offering yourself up to this deceptive female with both hands as a sacrifice for her to string you along, and if you're willing to be her highly attentive doormat after she disrespected you, why should she bother to hook up with you or go out on dates with you? All she has to do is keep blowing you off, and you'll keep simping for her faithfully.

Don't call or text the women who flake on you. Observe the rules of the game, and starve women of your attention and time whenever they flake on you. Don't call or text them unless they call or text you first.

Let's assume one of these flakes calls or texts you back. Don't get excited. Don't let her get too comfortable and start running off at the mouth. She flaked on you. That was some bullshit. Don't just accept this deceptive woman's bullshit. Take control of the conversation, and ask her why she flaked on you.

Allow her to explain. Give her enough rope to slip the noose around her neck before you kick the stool out from underneath her. Understand she's probably going to lie to you. Don't be naive to the fact that an indeterminable percentage of the world's sexually active female population are deceptive, cum-drinking, double-dick-clutching, two-faced sluts.

I don't point this out to be disrespectful. The game is what it is, women are who they are, and I point this out so you can place yourself in position to win whenever you deal with them. If all you want from this woman is casual sex, you shouldn't be all that concerned if she isn't honest and morally upright anyway. Especially if you're not honest and morally upright yourself. Don't be a hypocrite. You're trying to fuck her in every hole and come down her throat. What better way to use a beautiful liar?

Stay focused, allow her to explain why she flaked on you, and let her know she has to make things up to you for blowing you off. If you were supposed to hook up with her, tell her she's going to take you out for a drink at a spot of your choosing.

Don't ask her to do this. Tell her she's going to do this. Assume the drink. If you were supposed to go out on a date, tell her where she's taking you to eat. Tell her what day and time you're available to go out. Give clear instructions that are easy to understand and hold women accountable.

You're doing this to gauge her sexual interest in you. If she wants to see you and spend time with you, she shouldn't have any problems with your proposal. You shouldn't be super excited to spend time with a flake, but you want to see if she's going to redeem herself. If the flake agrees to hook up with you, or take you out on a date, cut the call short, give her specific instructions when to call or text you to confirm, tell her good-bye, and end the call.

Don't spend too much time on the phone with flakes. Too much chit-chat and small talk make you look like a clingy, needy, weak ass simp, and perception is reality in the game, unfortunately.

If the flake confirms and actually shows up to take you out, continue your campaign to get the pussy. If she flakes on you twice, it's apparent she has no interest in fucking you, charge her to the game, delete her contact information from your mobile, and never call or text her again.

Let's have a quick recap as this chapter draws to a close. Flaking, like rejection, is an inevitable, unavoidable part of the game. No man is safe from flaking, and no man is spared, but the rules of the game teach observant men how to deal most effectively with the women who flake on them.

Don't take flaking personally. Don't dwell on the goofballs who flake on you. Don't call or text them. If a flake calls or texts you back, tell her how she's going to make things up to you.

If she shows up and takes you out, (meaning she pays for the hook up or date), then continue campaigning for casual sex. If women flake on you and don't call or text you, don't call or text them either. Charge them to the game, and find more beautiful women to approach, hook up with, and date.

14 MAR 18 (WED)
1934/The Valley
The Cheesecake Factory, Sherman Oaks, California

CHAPTER 10

Be Yourself From The Beginning

I'm going to be myself. Say it with me. I'm going to be myself. Seven syllables roll off your tongue, and it sounds easy to do. Yet, if it truly were so simple for people to be themselves, we wouldn't have so many men and women going through their lives feeling empty, isolated, and unfulfilled because they have no idea who they are.

If you want to be yourself, you're going to have to learn who you are, understand who you are, and accept who you are. You have to accept yourself in order to be yourself.

The first step to learning the game is to develop your confidence. The second step is determining what you want from women sexually, and what you will and won't tolerate from them. The third step is to be true to the game and to be true to yourself at all times.

Learning who you are and learning to be yourself are not small endeavours, and I want you to understand this before you embark on the long journey inward. Self-discovery is a process which can take weeks. Or months. Or years.

It took me months to get in touch with who I am as a man, and I'm still learning who he is. People change every day. The same is true for you, so you'll always be learning something new about yourself. This is why you have to keep your mind clear, free, and open.

When I tell you to be yourself from the beginning, I'm encouraging you to be yourself and to be true to yourself from the first day you meet a woman to the last day you deal with her. Be yourself from the beginning when dealing with the women you want to fuck.

If you're hooking up with a woman for casual sex, take her to a bar or lounge you enjoy buying overpriced drinks from. Don't ask her where she wants to go. Take control of the hook up from the beginning.

If you're taking a woman out on a date, take her to a place where you enjoy the atmosphere, customer service, and the food. Engage in social activities you enjoy. Especially if you're paying for the date. Don't ask her where she wants to go. Take control of the date from the beginning.

This line of thinking flies directly in the face of the defective American social programming distributed through mass media, which helps to turn men into acculturated simps. This line of thinking flies directly in the face of so-called conventional wisdom which teaches men to place the happiness of women above their own.

I wrote this book to give my readers a much-needed change of perspective. Whenever you hook up with women or take them on dates, go to the places and do the things which please *you* and make *you* happy.

You're taking priceless time out of your life to read this book, so I offer this jewel of the game in return: Never go out of your way to impress women or make them happy. I don't care how pretty their faces are, how juicy their lips are, how big their tits are, how fat their asses are, how nice their thighs are, fuck all of that surface shit. Don't get caught up in the package when you're after the pussy. Never go out of your way to impress women or make them happy.

Some of you are going to disregard my advice because it challenges and defies what you've been taught about men, women, love, and sex by the people you respect most. I understand this. However, the people you respect most may not be able to give you the best advice and guidance you need in order to have casual sex with the beautiful women you desire.

If the people you respect most actually knew anything about the game and how to have casual sex with multiple comely women, they would never tell you to impress women and try to make them happy because they would already know that approach doesn't work.

Women aren't attracted to, nor are they sexually aroused by the men who try to impress them and make them happy. Some women will insist they adore men like this, but that's empty lip service. That's bullshit. An indeterminable percentage of women enjoy running game and exploiting naive men who are blissfully unaware of their true sexual nature. I'm here to warn you because I don't want you to fall for their fraudulent bullshit.

The men who try to impress women and make them happy aren't the men who get their pussies wet. In fact, if you're foolish enough to try that, they aren't going to appreciate your efforts. They're going to take you for granted, and expect you to keep running your fool's errand which is an exercise in futility.

You know what happens in the real world when you try to impress women and make them happy in order to fuck them? More often than not, those women will flake on you on hook ups and dates to go lick the balls and ride the dicks of full-dog alpha males, ladies' men, macks, players, and womanisers who never go out of their way to impress women or make them happy.

A beautiful woman isn't going to tell you this, but her pussy gets wetter than Niagara Falls in a Nor'easter when she's sexually attracted to a man, and she's completely into him, but he's not all that into her. He doesn't treat her like anything special.

He neglects her to a certain degree because she's not that important to him.

She's accustomed to men throwing themselves at her feet, but this new guy who she's really into doesn't do that. At all. It's a real challenge to capture his attention, and she can't stop thinking about this man. She's determined to pursue him. She can't help herself, and she's going to have casual sex with him if that's what it takes to capture his attention.

If you're hooking up with a woman, you're trying to take her back to your place or hotel/motel room and fuck her until the walls sweat. Hook ups are auditions where beautiful women want to see why they should have casual sex with you. Fuck these women with such force and passion they can't help but come back for more, but this is for your benefit. Not theirs.

Good sex is intoxicating, and it's easy to get drunk off the pussy. Enjoy yourself to the fullest, but don't allow sex to blind you or cloud your judgment. Sex is a harsh taskmaster, and she enslaves billions of people worldwide. It isn't your job to try and impress the women you want to have casual sex with and make them happy. Never forget this.

Men are socialised to become acculturated simps in the U.S., and simping can make one delusional, so I have to remind many of you that the women you want to hook up with aren't your girlfriends, nor are they your wives. You have no ties to these women. You just want to fuck them. Nothing more, nothing less. Therefore, don't make hook ups anything more than what they are, and understand your happiness comes first. Not theirs.

If you're taking a woman on a date, you're trying to get to know her a bit before you take her back to your place or a hotel/motel room and fuck her until the walls sweat. Dates aren't sexual auditions in the same way hook ups are, but the game is the same. It isn't your job to try and impress the women you want to date and make them happy. Never forget this.

You have no ties to the women you want to date. You want to spend some of your time and non-sexual companionship with them, which is fine but at the end of the day, you still want to fuck them. Therefore, don't make dating anything more than what it is unless a serious relationship comes from it. And even if that happens, remember your happiness always comes first.

Being yourself from the beginning, with the women you want to hook up with and date doesn't mean you should be disrespectful. I don't want any of you to misunderstand my words and misinterpret the game being shared here. If the women you're dealing with aren't being disrespectful and rude to you, then you have no reason to be disrespectful and rude to them.

If you're out with a woman and she disrespects you and gets out of line, you check the shit out of her right then and there. Don't hesitate. Don't think twice. Don't be nice. Let the impudent female know what the penalty for disrespect is right away.

However, if you're being disrespectful and rude with women for no reason, it sounds like you might have some pent-up anger and resentment you need to resolve. You'll also be the one going home alone with blue balls and a dry, hard dick. Does that sound like fun?

I knew some gentlemen of leisure when I lived in Detroit. One of them, a man I'll refer to as Al, observed me approaching women on the street. He advised me to "mix a bucket of cool and a bucket of smooth" when I stepped to the women I wanted to have casual sex with.

His unsolicited advice rankled me for two reasons: One, I thought my game with the hoes was pretty tight. Two, the natural bent of my intense personality was to be crude, curt, and direct.

I didn't see the value of Alfred's advice initially because I was arrogant, headstrong, and inexperienced in the game. I thought I knew better, but I also knew I wasn't fucking the beautiful women I desired on a consistent basis.

I knew I had potential in the game, but something stood in the way of my progress, and that something was me. I was stuck in my own way. I humbled myself, took Alfred's advice, and fucked five beautiful women at the gym where I worked out two weeks later.

If you're young (or not so young anymore), headstrong, and inexperienced in the game, I encourage you to take Alfred's advice to heart. It might not be your natural style, but your natural style might not be working for you. Or, your natural style might become much more effective with a few tweaks. Mix a bucket of cool and a bucket of smooth when you approach and flirt with the beautiful women you desire. It's okay if you're rough around the edges. I'm a bit rough around the edges myself, but I know how to be smooth long enough to fuck comely women.

Be yourself from the beginning when you meet women you want to hook up with and date. Take them where you want to go, and do the things you want to do when you chill with them. Let them get a glimpse and a taste of who you are.

I'm going to be myself from the beginning when I deal with the beautiful women I want to fuck. Say it with me. Twenty-six syllables roll right off your tongue, and it sounds easy to do because it is. Be yourself from the beginning. This is the easiest person for you to be because everyone else is already taken. Mix a bucket of cool and a bucket of smooth when you approach and flirt with the beautiful women you desire. Tell the dirty-minded women you want to fuck what you really want to do to them.

18 MAR 18 (SUN)
0307/The Valley
Mission Hills, Los Angeles, California

CHAPTER 11
A Word About Grooming And Dress

If you're a man who bathes, shaves, brushes, and flosses his teeth regularly, feel free to skip this chapter. You might find this information redundant and unnecessary. You might wonder what unwashed moron doesn't know all of this already. You might wonder why I wasted your time writing this chapter.

Feel free to move along.

My parents taught me to bathe daily with hot water and soap. They taught me to wash my hair regularly, to brush my teeth, floss and use mouthwash, to use deodorant, to clean and clip my fingernails and toenails. My father taught me to shave and go to the barbershop as a youngster. I maintain my personal hygiene this way as an adult, and I realise everyone wasn't raised to be this clean on a daily basis by their parent(s).

We weren't all raised the same way, nor were we all brought up with the same standards of grooming and dress. Life is what it is, and I'm not here to judge. I'm here to advise, encourage, and introduce tight game to men in need of it, so if you're seeking beautiful female casual sex partners in the U.S. (or any other industrialised country), there are some grooming and dress standards I admonish you to adhere to.

You could be blessed with the physical beauty of Adonis, and the honeyed charm of the Satanic serpent from the Garden of Eden who seduced Eve into eating the forbidden fruit;

but if you smell like a week's worth of ass funk, testicle sweat, and musty armpits, and you can't remember the last time you brushed your teeth, you're not going to get the pussy.

In fact, a prostitute might tell you to keep your money and refuse to fuck you until you clean yourself up. And I wouldn't blame the whore one bit. Offensive body odour and bad breath are instant pussy killers. Automatic turn-offs like no other.

Avoid instant pussy killers at all costs unless you actually enjoy not having casual sex with women. You're taking the time to read this book, so I find it safe to assume you don't enjoy not having sex.

You want some pussy. You want a beautiful female casual sex partner or two. Or ten. There are ways to dress, groom, and present yourself in order to attract and fuck the beautiful women you desire. Pay attention.

Grooming For Hook Ups And Dates

1. **Take a bath or shower before the hook up or date.** You want sex to happen. You want the woman to shed her clothes and get skin to skin with you, so take a bath or shower on the day of your hook up or date. If you're supposed to see your lady of interest at 8 p.m., I recommend bathing or showering at 5. Give yourself plenty of time to relax and get ready. Use hot water and soap, or a body wash with a neutral scent.

2. **Wash your hair. Use shampoo and conditioner.** Use a hairdryer, or give yourself enough time to let your hair air dry.

3. **Use deodorant or antiperspirant.** After you bathe and wash/dry your hair, don't forget to use deodorant or antiperspirant.

4. **Clean and clip your fingernails and toenails if necessary.** This is pretty self-explanatory. Women look at your hands more than you do, and you don't know what might turn her off. Clean and clip your fingernails and toenails if necessary. It could make the difference between you getting the pussy, or going home frustrated with blue balls and a dry, hard dick.

5. **Trim your beard/hair/moustache.** If you have skill and a steady hand, cut and trim your beard/hair/moustache with clippers, scissors, and trimmers. If you lack skill and a steady hand, make sure you see your barber before your hook up or date to get your facial features in order.

   This may sound insignificant, but, you want her to get butt ass naked and give you the pussy. Little things mean a lot in this game. Make sure you're clean and well-groomed when you show up for the hook up or date.

6. **Choose the hairstyle which gives you maximum confidence.** Hairstyles vary, and people love to be creative in how they express themselves and their personalities. Choose the hairstyle which makes you feel confident, sexy, and in complete control.

7. **Brush your teeth and floss.** Fresh breath is a must. For real, for real. She won't kiss you if you have shit mouth, okay? Make sure you floss first, brush your teeth, and use mouthwash, so you can show up for your hook up or date with fresh breath and a crisp mouthpiece.

8. **Go easy on the cologne.** Again, this is pretty self-explanatory. Don't suffocate women with your cologne. You have no idea how many men fuck up and overdo it with the fragrance. You don't have to spray on half the bottle. Give yourself a light spritz or two, and you're good to go. Less is more.

Dressing For Hook Ups

1. **Dress comfortably.** When you meet women for hook ups, dress comfortably. Hook ups are all about fun, easy, non-monogamous sex, and you want your attire to reflect and suggest this. Save your crisp business casual attire for dates instead.

2. **You can't go wrong with button down shirts and jeans.** I recommend button down shirts made of light, breathable fabrics like cotton. Wear jeans which make you feel confident, sexy, and in complete control. Dark denim jeans are always a winner, but if you're adventurous, you can sport a ragged pair of jeans with holes and rips. This is a revolving style which allows you to show some of your attitude and personality in your ensemble.

   Make sure your shirt is free of holes and stains. The ragged look works for jeans, not button down shirts. And make sure your shirt and jeans are clean because women will notice if they're not. They might not say anything, but they might not come back to your crib either. Follow the hook up dress code.

3. **T-shirts work too.** If a button down feels too formal for the occasion, you can opt for a t-shirt instead. T-shirts give you a much more relaxed appearance which may help to relax your hook up partner too. You can wear a blank tee without graphics, a tee from your favourite brand name designer, or a tee with your favourite band logo.

   I prefer black Cure t-shirts. I like the band, I like how I feel when I put a Cure t-shirt on, and it lets the woman I'm hooking up with know something about me and my taste in music without having to explain anything. Less said is best said. The full-dog alpha males, ladies' men, macks, players, and womanisers already know this. Make sure your t-shirt is clean and free from holes.

4. **My personal recommendation.** If I was hooking up with a beautiful woman on a Friday night, I would wear a black Cure t-shirt, slim, ripped black jeans, some black on black Vans Authentics, and a black Polo hoodie if the weather required me to don an outer layer. I keep my hook up attire comfortable, clean, and sexy because it's all about having fun, having some drinks, smoking some first-class indica, and having mind-blowing sex with no strings attached.

5. **Mobile etiquette.** Don't forget to put your mobile on silent. You don't want her looking down at her phone every two minutes, right? This would make you feel ignored and a bit neglected, correct? I thought so. Give her the same respect. Keep your attention focussed upon her, and put your mobile on silent.

Dressing For Dates

1. **Dress casually.** Don't dress for a hook up when you're taking a woman out on a date. Step your presentation up and follow the business casual dress code. Men dress up a bit for job interviews if they have serious interest in the position and the financial compensation being offered. Well, men with game and style dress up a bit for dates because they have serious interest in fucking the beautiful women they desire.

   The concept is the same. Don't dress too formally. You don't need to wear a suit and tie unless you're taking your date to the opera or the theatre. If you're taking a woman out to dinner and a movie, you're good with a blazer or a nice sweater.

2. **You can't go wrong with button down shirts and chinos.** I recommend button down shirts made of light breathable fabrics like cotton. Wear chinos or slacks instead of jeans,

and go with the pair which makes you feel confident and sexy. Make sure your pants are clean and free from holes and stains.

3. **Polo shirts work too.** If you don't like the button down look, you can opt for a Polo shirt instead. Leave your t-shirt at home. I don't care how cool you think it looks with your ensemble. Polo shirts are a business casual staple, they look good in most social settings, and you don't have to spend $98 on a Ralph Lauren Polo shirt. You can find more reasonably priced alternatives if you prefer.

   It's the business casual look and feel you're going for here. Make sure your shirt is clean and free from holes. Your date is going to try to find the imperfections in your appearance even while she's smiling and talking to you. Stay one step ahead of her and beat her at her own game.

4. **My personal recommendation.** If I was taking a woman out on a date, my attire would be blacked out like the New York City power outage of 1977. I would wear a black, slim-cut Polo blazer, black, slim-cut Polo shirt, black, slim-cut Polo chinos, some black and white socks, and I would complete the ensemble with a pair of black, big block gators.

   Black is the sexiest, most powerful colour in the known universe, and I want to exude confidence, power, and raw sex appeal for the length of the date in a subtle, stylish way. This is the fly shit. Allow your attire to speak for you and communicate your desire. I want my date to know I'm a man in all black, and I'm not for any of her bullshit. We're out drinking, eating, socialising, and spending some non-sexual time together, but I'm here to pound the pussy until the sun comes up.

   I keep my date attire clean, comfortable, dressy, sexy, and a bit dangerous because it's all about sending a charming, seductive impression which creates a hot, sexual image in your date's mind. It's all about having fun and showing her what her life could be like if she enters into a relationship with you.

5. **Mobile etiquette.** Don't forget to put your mobile on silent. You don't want her looking down at her phone every two minutes, right? This would make you feel ignored and a bit neglected, correct? I thought so. Give her the same respect. Keep your attention focussed upon her, and put your mobile on silent.

19 MAR 18 (MON)
1103/The Valley
Mission Hills, Los Angeles, California

CHAPTER 12

A Word About Shoes

Shoes complete your ensemble. Shoes express your attitude, status, and style. This is why you don't see homeless guys on Skid Row wearing alligator dress shoes, and you don't see investment bankers from Goldman Sachs wearing grimy, busted Chucks with holes in the soles. This just doesn't happen in the real world.

Shoes are the finishing touch. The cherry on top. If you're a man or a boy growing into manhood, you need to understand how important your shoe game is to your sex life, and how the right shoes can create sexual attraction between you and the ladies when you're out and about.

When women check you out to assess your potential sexual marketplace value, they're going to look at your shoes first. This is how they're going to form their first impression of you. If the ladies like what they see, they're going to work their way up from there. Shoes and sex are inextricably linked.

I included this chapter because I've seen too many men overlook and underestimate the importance of their shoes when they go out on hook ups and dates. They don't understand how women look at their shoes and make snap judgments about them in seconds.

One of the snap judgments a woman makes within seconds of first meeting a man is whether or not she's going to fuck him. Best believe your shoes play a part in how women are attracted to you if they're attracted to you at all.

If you're a man or a boy growing into manhood and you want to fuck multiple comely women, your shoe game has to be top-notch. You want women to distinguish you from the competition by your game and sense of style when they first see you, so keep reading, and I'm going to put you on to the basics of the shoe game for hook ups and dates.

You're going to see multiple references to the word 'effort.' When you're just hooking up with women, effort isn't as important. When you take women out on a first date, however, this thing called effort becomes magnified intensely and placed under the brightest spotlights like a blond, blue-eyed, A-List Hollywood star.

If you have no idea what I'm talking about, you might be a lame in the game who doesn't go on enough hook ups or dates. Whenever you hear women talking about men, first dates, and effort, they're referring to the fact women want to see men make an effort to impress them. Women interpret effort as respect. That's all effort means in this context. Got it? Good. On to the basics of the shoe game.

1. No trainers. I already know a lot of guys don't want to hear this. I understand. I already know this part of the game is going to go over like a lead balloon with an indeterminable percentage of guys in general, and an indeterminable percentage of brothers who adore wearing Jordans with every ensemble to every occasion in particular.

Jordans are dope trainers. Let's be real. A brand new pair of Air Jordans 3 Retro OG Black Cement fresh out the box are dope as fuck. I'll take two pair in size twelve. Jordans impress other guys who love the insanely popular luxury sneakers, there's an indeterminable segment of the male population who love competing against each other for female attention, and these are the guys who love to wear them.

Women aren't so impressed. If you show up for the first date in a pair of trainers, the woman is likely to assume you have poor taste, you're lazy, you didn't respect her enough to make a real effort for the date, and she's not going to get sexually aroused and interested in having casual sex with you.

I'm prone to have my own hard-headed, stubborn moments as well, but if you want to fuck the comely women you desire consistently, observe the rules of the game, and apply them to your life. Especially if you're not getting the results you want from doing things your way.

If you're hooking up with a woman, wear your Jordans if you wish. Hook ups don't have the same level of expectation or presentation. However, if you're meeting a woman for a first date, do yourself a favour, leave your trainers at home, and wear a pair of dressy, stylish, leather shoes.

Unless you're an NBA star. If you're a star player in the NBA, you can show up in a pair of Jordans for the first date. Or a pair of flip-flops for that matter. Women don't care about effort quite as much when you have a $200 million dollar contract.

2. Leave your boots at home if you don't live in horse country or cattle country. This doesn't apply to you if you're a guy who lives in Arizona. Or Montana. Or New Mexico. Or Oklahoma. Or Texas. Or Wyoming. Do you see where I'm headed with this? If you live in a region where cowboy boots are worn regularly as part of the local fashion, you might look a bit odd if you showed up for your first date without them.

This rule of the shoe game doesn't apply to you. Cowboys and ranchers are exempt. However, if you aren't a cowboy or a rancher and you don't live in horse country or cattle country, do yourself a serious solid and leave your boots at home. This also goes for all of my hip-hop heads and street n++++++ who take their Jordans off just long enough to slip on some Timberlands.

Timberlands are dope boots. Let's be real. A brand new pair of Timberland men's 6-inch premium waterproof boots in wheat nubuck fresh out the box are dope as fuck. I'll take two pair in size twelve. Be that as it may, I wouldn't wear a pair of Timbs on the first date because I'm not meeting my date at a construction site. Or a hip-hop video shoot.

You might think your boots make you appear tougher and more masculine, and she might think so too. But not on the first date. Not unless you live somewhere like Jasper, Texas, where it's as natural to wear shit kickers as it is to drive pickup trucks with Confederate flag bumper stickers and fully loaded shotguns in the gun racks, chain black men to the trucks by their ankles, and drag them for three miles until their bodies hit culverts and sever their heads and limbs like James Byrd, Jr. *Requiescat in pace.*

3. Save your sandals for pool parties and excursions to the beach. A lot of white guys are going to struggle with this one because the only people I've seen in the U.S. who like to have their toes out more than women are white guys. Asian men run a close second. I get that. However, if you're not meeting the woman for a hook up or a date at the beach or a pool party, leave your sandals at home and wear a pair of dressy, stylish, leather shoes instead.

If you choose to disregard the game and show up for the first date in sandals with your toes out, nine times out of ten, you're going to turn the woman off. Nine times out of ten, the woman is likely to assume you have poor taste, you're lazy, you didn't respect her enough to make a real effort for the date, and she's not going to get sexually aroused and interested in having casual sex with you.

This doesn't apply if you're in Oahu, Hawaii, and your first date is a picnic on the beach at sunset. Let's not forget to use a little bit of common sense. If your hook up or date is at the beach or a pool party, sandals are acceptable. Obviously. But if this isn't the case, and you're taking a woman out to dinner and a movie, leave your sandals at home.

Why?

Women don't want to see your toes out on the first date. They like looking at their own toes. Especially after they've just had a pedicure. They want to see you wearing a pair of dressy, stylish, leather shoes with a nice shine. This might seem silly to an indeterminable percentage of my readers, but it makes women feel like you made a real effort.

If you respect the game and practise its principles daily, you'll put yourself in position consistently to have casual sex with the beautiful women you desire. Your successful application of game-tested principles and strategies will distinguish you from the inferior competition, and women will notice this right off the bat.

Don't try to reinvent the wheel. You want to roll with the game like a brand-new Cadillac Escalade fresh off the lot, so follow these principles and watch how beautiful women react to you. You're welcome. Save your sandals for pool parties and excursions to the beach.

4. Wear dressy, stylish, leather shoes. Converse All-Stars and Vans are exceptions to this rule. Women like leather shoes. A lot. Perhaps they think leather shoes look nicer and offer higher quality than other types of shoes. You're not concerned with why women like leather shoes. Wear shoes women like on the first date so you can start building attraction from the moment you meet them.

Women will actually think you made a real effort to impress them. That's really all most sensible women are looking for on a first date, and this is exactly what you want them to think. If you've neglected your wardrobe and don't have a pair of dressy, stylish, leather shoes, you need to buy a pair. In black. Today.

Every man and boy growing into manhood needs to own at least one pair of dressy, stylish, black leather shoes. Converse Chuck Taylor All-Stars and Vans are notable exceptions to this rule because they're accepted as classic casual sneakers. If you prefer to wear Chucks or Vans on a first date, make sure they're clean and free from holes.

I wouldn't wear Chucks or Vans on a first date, but that's just me. My shoe game is serious like stage 4 cancer, and I don't fuck around because I know wearing the right shoes and speaking the right words can lead to me getting my dick sucked and fucking a beautiful, horny woman I just met.

This isn't hearsay, homie. I know this from personal experience, so I always dress accordingly, and I encourage you to do the same. You never know when you're going to meet a comely woman who wants to fuck you.

5. Dressy, stylish, leather shoes make you look like a sexy, masculine man in the eyes of women. I read on a blog somewhere that young men were concerned wearing stylish shoes would make them appear feminine. Or gay. I laughed out loud when I read that goofy shit, and almost sent the author an email to inquire which group of young men he was referring to specifically because I knew he wasn't referring to young black men from Detroit, Michigan.

I was born in the industrial slums of southwest Detroit. I grew up in its murderous, ghetto culture. I was nine years old when I knew I needed to wear expensive clothes, expensive shoes, and sexy fragrances if I wanted to fuck beautiful women. I knew this as a boy, and virtually every other black boy in Detroit knew this too because that's what our culture taught us.

The black men who black women in Detroit lusted after wore tailored business suits with razor-sharp creases and alligator dress shoes. They drove customised Cadillacs. They wore expensive jewellery. They carried guns. They hurt and murdered people occasionally. These men were drug dealers. Entertainers. Gangsters. Pastors. Pimps. Players.

Poor black boys in the slums grow up emulating those men and imitating their style of dress, which is one reason black men from Detroit are known as macks, pimps, and players around the world. Our reputation precedes us because we know how to dress and carry ourselves when we approach women to fuck them.

We know how to flirt with women verbally and physically to get them sexually aroused. We grow up in some of the most violent neighbourhoods in the U.S., yet we learn how to present ourselves to beautiful women and have casual sex with them from black players who are masters in the sexual arts of attraction, seduction, and manipulation.

So, I'm not sure who the author of that blog had in mind, but I want all men, young, middle-aged, and old alike, to understand that dressy, stylish, leather shoes make you appear sexy and masculine in the eyes of women.

When you wear dressy, stylish leather shoes, women perceive you as more mature, more sexually experienced, and able to defend them from physical danger should danger arise. Women infer all of this about men from the shoes they wear on the first date.

Making the effort to fix up and look sharp shows a man has confidence in himself, and nothing gets a woman's pussy wet like a confident, well-dressed man with nice shoes and inviting cologne who knows how to inject sex into his conversation. Seduction starts with hello.

6. Wearing dressy, stylish, leather shoes makes women think you made a real effort to impress them. Remember when I referred to effort earlier in the chapter? Good. You should have a clearer understanding of what I'm talking about now. Women interpret your effort as respect, and this is exactly what you want them to think.

The truth is, you should be up on your shoe game and wear nice shoes to please yourself, not women.

Don't buy expensive clothes and shoes and dress up to impress women. They will see right through your flimsy façade and spot the well-dressed, weak-minded simp under the fine fabrics. Buy expensive clothes and expensive shoes because you love yourself, you like yourself, you respect yourself, and you understand the need to put your best foot forward when approaching comely women for the fuckings.

Full-dog alpha males, ladies' men, macks, players, and womanisers get fly for themselves first and foremost. They put themselves first. The fact beautiful woman are impressed and attracted to them are secondary and tertiary. Do this for yourself first and foremost, and not for the beautiful women you want to fuck. This is what makes your game authentic and unique. This is what distinguishes you from your competition, and it all starts with your shoe game.

22 MAR 18 (THU)
0721/The Valley
Mission Hills, Los Angeles, California

CHAPTER 13

A Word About Housekeeping

Do you enjoy cleaning your home? Be honest. If your answer is yes, you fall within the peculiar, indeterminable percentage of the human population who actually enjoys cleaning their living spaces and feels a sense of accomplishment afterwards. My parents fall into this peculiar percentage.

They enjoy cleaning their home. They enjoyed cleaning their home so much they wanted to share that glorious experience with their children, so my siblings and I grew up cleaning the house every Saturday morning.

I shared my weekly drudgeries with four siblings, and our chores were completed promptly because we had old school parents from Alabama. Backtalk got rewarded with a smack in the mouth. We didn't talk back to them, and you wouldn't have said shit either.

Cleaning my place isn't my favourite activity by any stretch, but my parents forced me to do chores regularly. The chores became learned behaviour, I recognise when I need to tidy up, and I have the discipline to clean my place from top to bottom whether I have women coming over to fuck me or not.

Some of you reading this chapter weren't raised by parents who made you clean your homes religiously. Maybe you come from the higher socioeconomic class where people were paid to pick up after you. Perhaps you come from the lower socioeconomic stratum where you never had to tidy up because whoever raised you saw no need to keep a clean home.

Circumstances vary from person to person, but the bottom line is that some of you aren't so clean. This is apparent in your appearance and how your home looks and smells. This is why women find quick excuses to leave right after they enter your crib, look around and find sufficient evidence to safely assume they've stepped into the slovenly den of a fucking dirtbag.

Some of you reading this chapter already know how to clean up your place, and set a seductive mood where sex can pop off after you bring a woman home to hook up or cap a date off with a happy ending.

There's not much for you to see here, so you can move it along to the next chapter, or you can check out my housekeeping game, and see how you can keep your living spaces clean so sex can pop off anywhere in your home.

Your housekeeping game remains the same for hook ups and dates alike. You want women to get butt ass naked, suck dick, and fuck you. None of that has a great chance of happening if they come to your place and see you live in a pigsty. They're going to see you as a trifling pig, and women don't want to lie down with trifling pigs. They fuck rich pigs, but rich guys have people to clean up after them.

I didn't grow up with the luxuries and privileges of the rich, and if you didn't either, read the nine housekeeping deal-breakers which will practically guarantee women will not only not have casual sex with you, but they won't return for another hook up or date should you lose your good sense and choose to disregard this list.

1. Clutter. Believe it or not, this is an easy one for people to overlook for two reasons. One, clutter is a disordered heap or mass of objects. It doesn't look like filth, grime, or trash, so people tend to let clutter lie around and grow. Two, you might not look at your end tables, coffee table, dining room table, sofa, love seat, and floor as horizontal surfaces which need to be kept clean and free of clutter.

If the horizontal surfaces of your home aren't kept free of clutter, the disordered heaps and masses of objects can become a distraction which pulls your hook up partner's or date's attention away from you and the sexual mood you're trying to set. This is counter-productive to what you're trying to accomplish. You want the woman's attention on you. You want the woman's eyes on you.

Clutter includes blunts, books, cannabis, cigarettes, clothes, dishes, loose papers, magazines, mail, pencils, pens, silverware and other odds and ends you were too lazy to put away or throw away at the time. If you already know you're slow to clean up, factor this into your preparation time and take two to three days before your hook up or date is scheduled to get your place in order.

Women are always looking for your weakness(es). This is true even when they're grinning all up in your face with their big, fake tits pressed against your chest. Women grin in lots of guys' faces, so don't fall for that goofy shit like some jelly back, weak-minded simp.

Clean the clutter from your home. This might seem completely insignificant to you, but women will notice your clutter-free living spaces right away. Don't look for them to comment. They may not say anything to you, but this will distinguish you from all of the other dirtbag dudes they've hooked up with and dated. Women will see you in a different light, and it will help get them in the mood to fuck.

2. Dirty Laundry. Some of us are cleaner than others as we've already established, but we've all fallen behind on doing our laundry from time to time. It happens to the best of us, but the problem arises when dirty laundry hangs around too long, doubles or triples in size, and becomes funky ass laundry.

The stench of dirty laundry blends in with the other odours wrapped in your living spaces. You're accustomed to the smell(s) of your home, so you may or may not notice this. Your love interest isn't accustomed to how your home smells, so if she catches a whiff of the funky ass laundry you should have washed three weeks ago, the offensive odour could kill the mood quicker than racist, white supremacist police officers gunning down an unarmed, handcuffed black man in Anywhere, USA.

Your hook up partner or date will assume you're a fucking dirtbag, she'll quickly find a reason to leave, and you'll be home alone, pissed off, beating your dick while she goes to suck and fuck the next man who knows how to do his laundry.

Don't be lazy and hide your dirty laundry in a closet a couple of hours before your hook up or date takes place. Don't practise dusty behaviour. It's best to do your laundry once a week to stay on top of it. Doing laundry once every two weeks is stretching things a bit, but it's still manageable.

Waiting a month to a month and a half or longer to do laundry is entering into dusty n+++++ country. That isn't where you want to be. If you already know you hate doing this particular chore, take your displeasure into account, split it into separate loads, and wash your funky ass laundry two to three days before your hook up or date takes place.

Don't forget to wash your bath towels and hand towels. Women you bring back to your place will ask to use your bathroom because they want to see how clean it is. The last thing you want is for the woman to wash her hands and grab a hand towel which smells like your ass. Or your roommate's ass.

It's good manners to have clean bath towels and hand towels available for guests. That's just being a good host. Make the effort for a beautiful woman you want to fuck, homie. Wash your bath towels and hand towels with your laundry. You're welcome.

3. Dirty Sheets. This one is an instant hook up-ender. An instant pussy killer. Listen, it's no small feat to bring a woman back to your crib. That's a victory in itself. It's even tougher to get a woman in bed. It takes game, confidence, and seductive charm to make that happen.

It takes work to get women in bed, and you don't want to let all of your game and effort go to waste because you were either too absent-minded, too dusty, or too lazy to wash your dirty sheets. You'll be angry with yourself afterwards, and I know this from personal experience.

Something as small and inconsequential as potato chip crumbs on your sheets can turn women off. And women are funny, okay? They know you have sex in your bed, but they don't want to see any incriminating physical evidence of the sex you've had with other women.

Incriminating physical evidence could be a smear of lipstick or makeup on your sheets. Sweat stains. A strand of another woman's hair. Cum stains. Don't go against the grain, gentlemen. Do yourself a huge favour, and wash your sheets the night before or change them on the day of your hook up or date.

If a woman brings a man home for casual sex after a date or a hook up, and she's halfway attractive with a fat ass, slim waist, nice thighs, and big tits, he doesn't give two fucks about her sheets. He might not notice unless her linen is soiled. If he's on his game, he's focussed on dicking her down and stroking the bottom of her pussy so he can provide multiple orgasms. If he's on his game, he's focussed on fucking her into submission.

Thoroughly satisfying sex puts her to sleep like nature's sweetest sedative, and if he spends the night, he will wake up to breakfast in bed with the woman staring down at him. I've seen this look more times than I can count. When a woman looks at you in this curious way, she's trying to determine how she can snare your heart and keep your dick in her pussy.

A woman gets a most peculiar gleam in her eyes when a man fucks her the right way. The poor girl might be dickmatised if the homie fucked her with no mercy. An indeterminable percentage of men may not be terribly concerned about dirty sheets, but women are very different from us. They do care about such things, and you care about fucking the pussy and converting comely women into disciples of your dick, so don't forget to wash your sheets.

4. Filth/Grime. Bathrooms and kitchens have the potential to become the filthiest, grimiest rooms in anyone's home because people don't like cleaning them. Men have a bit of an advantage here because women don't expect us to be as clean as they might be.

She isn't expecting your home to meet the standards of hospital cleanliness, but she certainly doesn't want to step in your bathroom and be greeted by pubic hairs on the floor, facial hairs in your sink from your last shave, a toothpaste stained mirror, an overflowing trash can, piss on your toilet seat, and a corn-studded turd floating in the toilet.

Women don't want to step into your kitchen and be greeted by the stench of refuse and rotting food in your garbage can you should have emptied three weeks ago. Women don't want to see your greasy counters, greasy stove, and dirty dishes with caked-on food (or mouldy food) stacked in your unclean sink with a cockroach on top.

Having a filthy bathroom and kitchen is unacceptable. Especially when you have a housekeeping advantage which was cooked into the culture centuries ago. The average American woman doesn't expect you to be as clean as she might be.

She knows you're a man. She just wants to see if you made an effort to impress her for the hook up or date, and nine and a half times out of ten she's not going to tolerate your filthy bathroom and grimy kitchen.

And she shouldn't. Not for half a second. Any woman with a decent amount of self-esteem should walk right out on a guy who's too lazy and dusty to clean his bathroom and kitchen before he invited her over to fuck him. It takes a lot of game, confidence, seductive charm, and work to get women back to your place, so don't blow your opportunities to have casual sex with them.

5. No air conditioning/heat. This may sound hard to believe, but I've given advice to women in the dating game, and more than a few of them told me how they hooked up with and dated guys who refused to adjust the air conditioning/heat to make them more comfortable. This isn't hard to figure out, guys. This might actually be the easiest deal-breaker to fix on the list.

When you bring women back to your place for casual sex, you need to create a sexy, inviting atmosphere that gets them aroused, and makes them want to fuck you. That makes sense, right? I live in LA, so I don't have to worry about turning the heat up very often. Air conditioning hits homeowners and renters in their pockets because it's hot nine months out of the year in sunny SoCal.

Don't worry about saving money on your electric bill to the point you refuse to adjust your air conditioning/heat to accommodate your hook up partner or date and make her feel comfortable enough to have casual sex with you. You might save a few pennies, but she could leave you at home with a dry, hard dick, and you can't fuck your electric bill, okay? Don't be a miserly simp. Adjust your air conditioning/heat accordingly when you have women over.

6. Offensive Odours. Offensive odours kill the mood faster than Jack the Ripper disembowelling whores in the piss-run alleys of Whitechapel, London, England, in 1888. We become oblivious to the odours in our homes because we spend so much of our time there, but your hook up partner or date will not be oblivious to how your home smells.

Don't try to smother the funk in your home with air fresheners. Odours collect in your carpet, so make sure you vacuum the carpeted surfaces in your home before your hook up or date takes place. Sweep and mop your bathroom and kitchen with soap and hot water. I also burn incense. It helps create the mood I like to set, and I like the smell of it combined with the indica. I'm not suggesting you burn incense (or smoke weed) if you're not already in the habit of doing so, but make sure you get rid of the offensive odours in your place.

7. Pets. Disciplined, well-groomed, well-maintained pets don't kill the mood on hook ups and dates. A disciplined, well-groomed, well-maintained, pet is a conversation starter which could draw women closer to you. Especially if they love animals. The white women that I've dealt with were huge animal lovers. An indeterminable percentage of them seem to care for animals far more than they love people, but I digress...

Disciplined, well-groomed, well-maintained pets don't kill your hook up partner's or date's mood to have casual sex with you. Poorly kept pets who lack discipline and grooming can definitely kill the mood. Women will look at your unkempt pet(s) and question your cleanliness and character. Excessive cat or dog fur on your furniture, paw prints on counters and floors, and stinky litter boxes are all red flags. Clean up after your pet(s) thoroughly on the day of your hook up or date.

8. Questionable Material. What you do in your home is your business, and it's a good idea to keep it that way on the first hook up or date. I respect the boundaries of others, and I demand others respect mine in return.

Maybe you like guns. Maybe you go to the shooting range regularly, you own multiple firearms, and you're completely immersed in the gun culture. That's cool, but I wouldn't have any of my firearms on the coffee table when my hook up partner or date walks into my home for the first time. You have guns. If you're not in law enforcement, the military, or organised crime, that might be too much to share on the first hook up or first date.

Maybe you like cocaine. I used to like coke once upon a time too, but I wouldn't have a few lines cut on my glass coffee table when my hook up partner or date walks into my home for the first time. You like playing in the snow. That's cool, but that might be too much to share on the first hook up or first date.

This doesn't apply if you're a coke dealer, or if you met your hook up partner or date while snorting rails in a bar bathroom, at a club, concert, house party or wherever you met her. If you met a woman while you were getting blowed, there's nothing to hide. If this isn't the case, keep it out of sight. The same goes for heroin, meth, opioids, or whatever else you might be into.

Maybe you like porn. That's cool. Pornography is a part of every day life in America, but this doesn't mean you need to have it out in plain sight for the first hook up or date. If you haven't discussed drugs, guns, and pornography with the woman coming over, don't assume she's going to be comfortable with any of it.

In truth, she might be quite comfortable with drugs, guns, pornography, threesomes, whips, chains, and BDSM. You might have hit the fucking jackpot, homie, but have that talk first. You don't want her to make assumptions about you and what you're comfortable with, so give her the same respect.

9. Trash. There isn't much to say about this because there's no excuse to have trash strewn about your home. If your hook up partner or date sees overflowing trash cans and wastebaskets, she's going to make a mental note you're a lazy dirtbag. She's not going to tell you this. You just won't see her again.

Women will seek your weaknesses at every turn. There are women who will use trash as a reason to get distracted on the hook up or date. Those dirty tissues on your coffee table you think nothing about can become a distraction.

Those empty potato chip bags, food wrappers, take-out boxes, liquor bottles, and beer cans scattered about your crib are ammunition women can use as distractions to front on you and not give you the pussy. Don't give them that option. Clean your place and pick your trash up. You want clean, empty trash cans when women come over to your place to fuck.

27 MAR 18 (TUE)
1325/The Valley
Mission Hills, Los Angeles, California

CHAPTER 14

The Best Way To Get Beautiful Women Back To Your Place

Whether you want to just hook up with women for casual sex, or date them in either short-term or long-term monogamous or non-monogamous romantic relationships, your ultimate desire and objective are the same. You want to fuck the beautiful women you desire. Millions of men dream of this. You need to realise there are millions and millions of women who want to have casual sex too, but multitudes of men still fail to understand and grasp this simple truth.

If you're one of those men who just can't bring himself to believe millions of women enjoy casual sex just as much as men do, you're delusional. I'm not sorry to break the bad news to you, and I recommend you read my blog and my books until you realise you're living in a fantasy and snap the fuck out of that goofy shit.

I'm not going to belabour the point here, but don't deceive yourselves, brethren. There are women who enjoy casual sex just as much as men do, and this is why it's not hard to get them back to your crib and fuck them. Back when the United States Armed Forces used to actually win wars, a large part of their success came from logistics and how they deployed force in the field with lethal efficiency. Good logistics play a major role in hook ups and dates as well.

Proximity is everything. It's much easier to get women back to your place if you meet them at a bar or lounge no more than five to ten minutes walking distance from either your home or the hotel/motel room you're taking them to.

If you don't want women to know where you live, then I recommend getting a hotel/motel room. Be very careful who you allow into your home. An indeterminable percentage of these women are treacherous, and you don't want them to know where you lay your head at night.

Seduction starts at hello, so start flirting with her as soon as you sit down. Generally speaking, a woman knows whether or not she's going to sleep with a man within ninety seconds to three minutes after she meets him.

An indeterminable segment of the male population refuses to embrace this truth, but women already know whether or not they're going to fuck men when they meet them, so there's no need to be shy. You want to know where you stand, so start flirting with her as soon as you sit down and order the first round.

Flirt verbally and physically. Talk about sex. Start seducing her right away because you're only going to be at the bar or lounge for forty-five minutes to one hour tops before you tell her it's time to go. You don't have long to flirt and build the sexual tension in your attempt to persuade her to have casual sex with you.

You're probing her level of sexual interest to see if she's going to flake. This is where the rubber meets the road. Remember, she's already decided if she's going to fuck you or not, so you're trying to see if you can get the pussy that night.

Some women may act offended when you speak to them in such a direct, sexual manner. That's fine. Don't apologise. Don't back down. Letting a woman know you're interested in having sex with her is not sexual assault, sexual harassment, or rape. When you sit down, take her by the hand, make eye contact and say, "You have pretty eyes. Has anyone ever told you that?"

She will nod or say yes.

You will then say, "I thought so. When's the last time he made you climax?"

Wait for her response. Nine times out of ten she's going to laugh. You were sexual without being profane, and this is going to catch her off-guard. Let her go if she objects and leaves. Don't waste another drop of your energy, another cent of your money, or another second of your time on uncooperative women who don't want to have casual sex with you. Charge those women to the game.

If she laughs, that's a good sign. Proceed. Keep talking about how you're going to make her orgasm and escalate your physical flirting. This is how you build sexual tension. Go from holding her hand to touching her arm. Let your fingers linger there for a moment or two.

If she doesn't object to your physical escalation, she likes how you're flirting with her and making her feel. Women go with how they feel in the moment, and you want to go with that. Escalate. Move from her arm to her knee. If she doesn't object, touch her thigh.

Don't be afraid. If she doesn't stop your physical escalations, keep flirting, drinking, and touching her until you start kissing and making out. Make out for a while, and tell her it's time to leave. Pay your bar tab, take her by the hand, and go back to your place or your hotel/motel room. If she's interested in you and you followed my advice to the letter, she should be ready to go.

If she refuses to go with you, recognise the game she's playing. An indeterminable percentage of the women you're going to meet are conniving, double-dick-clutching frauds and liars who aren't going to tell you they have boyfriends. They're not going to tell you they're married.

They're not going to tell you they live with their fiancés they've been engaged to for the last six years. There's an indeterminable percentage of women who are honest enough to tell you the truth, but more often than not, women will lie just like men do. Just like you might lie whenever it suits you best. Don't try to force her to leave with you. Don't force yourself upon women.

There is no room for rape, sexual assault, and sexual harassment in the game, so pay your bar tab and leave if the woman doesn't cooperate with you. Don't call or text uncooperative women. Let them contact you, and you can decide if you want to deal with them. I don't recommend dealing with goofy ass flakes, but if you choose to give such women a second chance, they have to make things up to you by taking you out, paying for the hook up or date, and fucking you.

If a woman who flaked on you isn't willing to do that, delete her contact information from your mobile so you can't contact her anymore. Don't fuck with her anymore. Recognise she has no real sexual interest in you, she's trying to play you and string you along for whatever you're stupid enough to give her, so charge that corny ass, manipulative, self-serving bitch to the game and continue your campaign with other beautiful women.

If the woman cooperates and goes back to your crib or hotel/motel room, you're one step closer to getting the pussy, but that's no guarantee you're going to have casual sex with her. You need to understand this. You need to understand women can say no and refuse sex even after you bring them back to your place. You can get her butt ass naked, and she can say stop. You can be balls deep up in a woman, and she can change her mind.

There are men doing time in prison because they didn't stop when women asked them to. Don't become one of those guys. Stop if a woman asks you to stop, let her get dressed, leave, and don't contact her again. Delete her contact information from your mobile, and charge her to the game. Discard all uncooperative women in this manner.

If she goes back to your place or hotel/motel room, gets butt ass naked, and fucks, let me be the first to congratulate you. She could still be married or have a boyfriend or a fiancé, but there's no need to ask her about that.

Less said is best said. You're here to have casual sex with the beautiful women you desire, not run background checks. The game is real, too many of these women lie like they fucking breathe, so stay on point like bayonets. Let's have a quick recap as this chapter draws to a close. What's the easiest way to get beautiful women back to your place?

1. Consider logistics. Meet them at a bar no more than five to ten minutes walking distance from your place or hotel/motel room.
2. Start flirting as soon as you sit down. Inject sex into the conversation. Let them know you're interested in having casual sex to see if they're sexually attracted to you.
3. If they're uncooperative, end things quickly, and find more beautiful women to approach for casual sex.
4. If they're cooperative and sexually attracted to you, flirt with them physically and verbally. Escalate by touching them while you talk.
5. If they don't stop your physical escalations, keep flirting, drinking, and touching them until you start making out. Make out with them for a while, and tell them it's time to go.
6. Don't press the point with uncooperative women who don't want to leave with you. Don't force yourself on

women. Pay your bar tab, leave them right there in the bar or lounge, and don't contact them again.

7. If the women are cooperative and ready to go, take them back to your crib or hotel/motel room, get naked and fuck the shit out of them. Congratulations!

8. Understand women can flake and tell you they don't want to have sex with you even after you've already entered the pussy. Understand this is part of the game, and it can happen to you. Stop if women ask you to stop, let them get dressed, leave, and never contact them again. Charge all uncooperative women to the game. For real, for real. Don't give them any opportunities to play you twice.

28 MAR 18 (WED)
2145/The Valley
Mission Hills, Los Angeles, California

CHAPTER 15

First Date

Human beings spend their lives in a tug-of-war with their emotions. Sometimes we can remain in control of our feelings and thoughts, and at other times, we simply cannot. Whenever we lose control, we surrender ourselves to our essential, primal natures and go down whatever dark, winding road our emotions decide to take us. These are the moments when we are most human.

This helps to explain why an indeterminable percentage of white American sports fans get drunk and high, then riot, overturn cars, set fires, and vandalise private and public property in blazing revelries to celebrate championships won by their favourite sports teams.

The drama, passion, and violence of sports plus the heady combination of alcohol and narcotics stir barbaric, destructive emotions and impulses within an indeterminable percentage of aggressive, loony fucking white people who have a disturbing obsession with athletics.

This also helps to explain why full-dog alpha males, ladies' men, macks, players, and womanisers can meet women, flirt with them, seduce them, and have casual sex with them (be it anal, oral, vaginal, or all three) within twenty to thirty minutes of meeting them for the first time. Bear in mind an indeterminable percentage of these women are the fiancées, girlfriends, and wives of other men.

Their relationship statuses are inconsequential because the indomitable arrogance, intoxicating confidence, and raw sex appeal of dominant, handsome, muscular men stir whorish lusts and slutty fascinations deeply embedded within the hearts, minds, and spirits of sexually active women worldwide.

Women go with their feelings when they deal with men sexually, and this often remains true even when their overpowering erotic pull goes against their better judgment.

This is why you can have casual sex with a woman twenty to thirty minutes after you meet her if you know how to read her body language quickly and correctly, how to flirt, and how to bring the sexual tension to a boil while creating an atmosphere where she feels comfortable kissing, touching, sucking and fucking you.

Women go with their feelings because this is when they're happiest. This is when they feel the freest, so the best time to have sex with a woman is within the first twenty-four to forty-eight hours of meeting her. This is when sex will be most spontaneous.

Once you edge past the seventy-two-hour mark, the wonder glow of meeting you begins losing its lustre and starts wearing off, so you want to fuck the beautiful women you desire before this happens.

The next time you approach a beautiful woman, pay close attention to her body language. If she steps back when you approach her, she's probably not interested. You're going to have to talk some marvellous shit to warm her up to you. And it still might not work.

If she doesn't move at all, she's indifferent. She's not repulsed by you, but she's not all up in your face either. You have a fifty-fifty shot basically, and you can't ask for better odds if your game is tight. If she moves toward you when you approach her, she's interested in hearing what you have to say. There's a chance she might like you too.

Let's say you approached this woman and she moved toward you. Take her by the hand. If she doesn't pull her hand back, she's comfortable with this level of physical contact. Learn to recognise when women are cooperating with you. Look for the unspoken signs early.

If she doesn't take her hand back, she's cool with what you've initiated. Don't hesitate. Start talking about casual sex. Tell her she has a two-hour opening to exchange orgasms back at your place.

Be bold. Don't worry about what she might say. There are millions upon millions of women just waiting for men to boss up and approach them for casual sex in such a straight-forward fashion.

This approach is not for the timid or faint of heart. The woman you desire could curse you out in two languages. She could laugh in your face. She could say no. She could say yes.

I want to reinforce the message that you don't have to take women out on dates in order to fuck them. Try to get the pussy when you first meet beautiful women you desire, and this is the best approach because you're letting them know it's all about casual sex straight from the gate.

However, if you prefer to take the long way to the pussy by taking women out on dates, knock yourself out. It's your energy, money, and time you're investing, whether you invest them wisely or foolishly, but you want to maximise every dating opportunity you create for yourself, so read the ten first date strategies listed below. They will increase your player efficiency, and prevent you from wasting your energy, money, and time on deceitful, attention-whoring females.

Dennis Park's First Date Strategies:

1. You will never see most of these women ever again after the first date. Someone needs to tell you this before you take random women out to dinner and the movies on first dates, spend way too much money on them, repeat this cycle for a few more dates, and never hear from them again. This is how men with little to no game with women get played into spending money without fucking. This is exactly what you're trying to avoid.

Dating is a numbers game. You have to approach a lot of women. Most of those women are going to find a reason to flake on you after the first date. It doesn't matter how tight you think your game is. They're going to find a reason to flake on you, and you're never going to see them again. There are reasons for this.

An indeterminable percentage of the women you're going to meet are going to be married. An indeterminable percentage of the women you meet are going to have fiancés. Boyfriends. Girlfriends.

An indeterminable percentage of the women you're going to meet might not be in established romantic relationships per se, but they live with their lovers for economic stability. A lot of these women are fucking and pursuing other men while they're dating and hooking up with you. It doesn't really matter why women flake on you after the first date. The truth is you're not going to see them again, and this is why it makes no sense to invest too much of your energy, money, and time into first dates.

2. Keep your first dates short and inexpensive. We've already established most of the women you date are going to flake on you after you take them out once. If you happen to be rich (and famous), this might not be the case, but be aware that the women you're dealing with are probably much more enamoured with your social status and wealth than you as a man. Don't delude yourself. An indeterminable percentage of women in the U.S. are raised to be acculturated prostitutes for men with wealth, power, and privilege. It's the culture of the country.

If you're like the overwhelming majority of men in the U.S., however, you're neither rich nor famous. You're not in the elite class and you never will be. It's a challenge to pay the rent sometimes, so you don't have disposable income to waste on manipulative liars who are only out for themselves. Keep your first dates short and inexpensive.

Your first dates should last no more than one hour, and you shouldn't pay any more than $25.00 to $35.00. You'll distinguish yourself from your competition immediately because you're not giving her a lot of your attention, and you're not spending a lot of time with her upfront like the simps she's accustomed to. You have sixty minutes to ascertain whether this woman is worth your time and money to fuck with her. Charge her to the game and move on to the next if she's not.

You want the first date to last an hour or less because the longer the date goes, the more the woman will expect you to spend on her. Fuck that stupid shit. You don't know this woman from a fucking hooker working the Diamond Inn off of Sepulveda and Parthenia in North Hills.

This is just the first date, and you might never see her again, so don't put her up on a pedestal because you'll only be angry at yourself for doing so later. Don't give any of these women too much credit. They're just as human as you are. Keep your first dates one hour or less, spend no more than $25.00 to $35.00, and try to get women back to the crib.

Try to get the pussy on the first date. This isn't the time to be a gentleman. Let her know you want to fuck. She might decline your invitation, and she has every right to do so, but don't contact her again if she doesn't kiss you on the first date. You need to feel some tongue, and you need to cup some ass.

If women can't do that much, they're showing you they have little to no sexual interest in you. Take the hint, don't play yourself, and don't fuck with women who won't kiss you on the first date. Fuck them. Charge them to the game, and move on.

3. Don't take women out to dinner and a movie on the first date. I understand if it sounds like a good idea for you to take a woman out to dinner and a movie on the first date. This is what you've been conditioned to accept and believe from all of the movies and TV shows you've seen. It's not your fault that American society is fraught with simpery, but you shouldn't take a woman out to eat in a nice restaurant until you've fucked her the way you want to at least twenty times.

We just established you're going to meet attention-whoring women with baby daddies, boyfriends, fiancés, girlfriends, and husbands. Are you really trying to feed those crafty bitches? Especially when they could flake on you at any time? Don't be stupid. You aren't in the game to give women your attention, time, free alcohol, and free meals.

A blunt walk is a cool first date. Let's say I have a first date at Santa Monica State Beach. I'm going to roll the blunt, we're going to take a stroll down the beach, and we're going to talk. If I don't like her vibe by the time I'm done smoking, the date is over. There's no reason for me to feed her, waste money, and waste anymore of my time, so we part ways, I delete Miss Whatever's contact information, and I approach another comely woman for casual sex if she's fly enough to catch my eye.

However, if I like the vibe I'm getting from Miss Whatever, I'll take her to grab some burgers and fries, and I'm not spending more than $25.00 to $35.00. I don't care if she's a professional swimsuit model. Treat all of the women you deal with the same, and don't put any of them up on pedestals. Don't waste your energy, money, and time on women who might not even like you.

If I still like the vibe by the time the meal is done, I'll roll another blunt and invite her back to the crib for a nightcap. Don't take women out to nice restaurants and foot expensive bills if you haven't fucked them the way you want to at least twenty times. Don't play yourself.

4. Pay attention to the women who pay of their own volition. This part of the game is crucial and overlooked. Let's say you take your date to a bar and she buys drinks without you asking her to do so. Take note of that. You might want to take her out on a second date if the vibe is right.

Why? Most of the women you take out on first dates aren't going to volunteer to pay for shit. If a woman spends money on the first date of her own volition, it says something about her character, and it also shows she likes you. She's cooperating and playing her part.

You're going to encounter an indeterminable percentage of women who expect you to pay for everything on dates just because you're a man. Never mind these women haven't fucked you and have no intentions on ever doing so. They still expect you to entertain them and spend your hard-earned money on their amusement. Fuck that. Don't be dumb enough to fall for their bullshit. Pay attention to the women who pay of their own volition.

5. Women who like you will cooperate from the beginning, and they won't mind paying their share. The women who like you will cooperate with you right from the beginning, and they won't mind paying the tip or paying for half of the date. Women who enjoy being around you will cooperate because they like how they feel when they're with you. They don't want that feeling to stop.

It's not easy to meet the women who like you because hooking up with and dating beautiful women is a numbers game. It's the luck of the draw, really. It's a roll of the dice, but it's so fucking cool when you meet beautiful women who are attracted to you sexually.

Everything goes so smoothly it seems surreal, at times. You'll know when it's happening because beautiful women you just met will laugh at your jokes, they'll buy drinks of their own volition, they'll cooperate when you flirt, they'll make out when you initiate, they'll go home with you gladly, and they'll fuck your fucking brains out.

6. Don't go on dates if you can't afford to. Don't be a dumbass. This is self-explanatory. If it's a struggle to spend $25.00 to $35.00 on a first date and you really can't afford it, taking women out and trying to get some pussy shouldn't be your first priority. Make sure you have all of your bills and living expenses covered for the month with some disposable income left over before you take women out on dates and hook ups. A cool, cooperative woman may help with the bar tab, but don't expect her to help pay your rent, utilities, and other living expenses. Don't go on dates if you can't afford to. Don't be a dumbass.

7. Fuck if women think you're cheap. Fuck what they think. Gentlemen, I cannot stress this enough. Most of the women you take out on first dates are going to flake on you. It makes no sense to waste your energy, money, and time trying to impress women who want to take all of the attention, free alcohol, free food, and time they can get from you and give you nothing in return.

Western women have been conditioned to expect men to pay for everything on dates which is bad enough, but an indeterminable percentage of these privileged, self-centred, thankless sluts and whores have the nerve to complain if they feel men didn't spend enough to entertain them. Fuck what those women say, and fuck what they think. It's not your job to spend money on women and impress them.

If you live on the Pacific Coast or in the Southwest, you can take a woman to In-N-Out Burger on a first date and get burgers, fries, and soft drinks for two for under $25.00.

If that's not good enough for a woman you just met, and she has the nerve to talk shit, be glad that's all you spent to find out what type of woman this ungrateful bitch really is, delete her contact information from your mobile, charge her to the game, and don't ever call or text her again. Let her find some pathetic, jelly back, weak-minded simp who's more than willing to waste his attention, energy, money, and time on her, and not get any pussy.

It's not your job to spend money on women in attempts to impress them. If a woman thinks you're cheap and is rude enough to say so, that's the very last time you should see or speak with the ungracious slattern. Stick to your guns, and spend no more than $25.00 to $35.00 on first dates. Fuck if women think you're cheap. Fuck what they think.

8. Don't try to make women like you. Charge them to the game if they're uncooperative. Women who don't cooperate with you romantically and sexually don't like you. They don't want to date you or have sex with you. A lot of them are looking for attention and nothing more because they already have men who help them financially and satisfy their sexual needs.

These women aren't going to tell you the truth, an indeterminable percentage of them have lovers at home, so don't become so desperate for female companionship and physical contact that you slip and play yourself. You aren't here to make women like you. That's a fool's errand.

You're in the game to fuck the comely women who make your dick hard for as little energy, money, and time spent as possible. Assume control of the date from the moment you say hello. If you catch a bad vibe on the first date, don't be afraid to end things right then and there. Immediately. Don't try to make any of these women like you, and charge them to the game if they aren't cooperating with you to the fullest.

9. Don't allow a woman to change the date you've planned unless she's paying for the date she's proposing. Women are always looking for your weakness(es). This includes an indeterminable percentage of women who want to see if you're soft enough to let them hijack control of the date you're expected to pay for. Don't allow a woman to change the date you've already set and planned out unless she's paying for the new date she's proposing.

If you're paying for the date, this gives you the power to call the shots, and she's free to follow your lead. Cancel if she objects to this, and don't contact her again. Simple as that. Don't allow a woman to change the date you've planned unless she's paying for the date she's proposing.

10. Ask her to come back to your place. If the first date goes well, you should spend an hour getting to know her a little better, and you should spend no more than $25.00 to $35.00. If everything is cool when the date comes to a close, invite her back to your place for a drink.

Don't be surprised if she declines. In truth, the woman may want to go back to your place and fuck your brains out, but she might not give you the pussy because she's not sure how you're going to look at her after your first casual session is over. Women know an indeterminable percentage of men become envious, insecure, possessive, and treat them differently after sex.

Invite her back to your place because you want to her to know you want to fuck. You don't want there to be any misunderstandings. If she says no, casual sex could happen on the second date or the third, but it most likely won't happen at all if you don't put your bid in. Don't be afraid to let these women know you want to fuck.

30 MAR 18 (FRI)
1821/The Valley
Mission Hills, Los Angeles, California

CHAPTER 16

Second Date

The first date was a pleasant surprise at the end of a rough week. There was great chemistry from hello, and conversation flowed like the Mississippi River without any awkward first date moments. You invited her back to the crib. Miss Comely declined, but her kiss was deep, long, and slow. You grabbed her ass. Lust heated up quick like chicken grease in a deep fryer, but she broke your embrace, told you she wanted to see you again, and now you have a second date.

It's cool your first date went well, but don't romanticise the experience. Don't make more out of it than what it was. The second date is where an indeterminable percentage of gameless, inexperienced men unwittingly set themselves up for failure by putting themselves and their happiness second to the women they desire.

This indeterminable percentage of gameless, inexperienced men believe not putting their happiness first impresses women, and increases their chances of fucking them. These men fail to realise they're building a weak foundation from the outset, and they won't recover from this dicey position.

When you put yourself second to women you want to fuck, you tell them they're more important than you are. You assure them their happiness outweighs yours. You're deferring to women you don't know in the feeble hopes they appreciate your selfless sacrifice, shower their affections upon you, and serve you the pussy with both hands. Deference is a form of communication, and communication is a two-way street. Whenever you send women the message they're more important than you are, you also relay that message to yourself simultaneously.

Those unspoken messages set the wrong precedent from the beginning, they sabotage your progress moving forward, and the worst part is you probably have no idea this is happening. This is why you're confused and sexually frustrated when the beautiful women you want to fuck banish you to the dreaded friend zone with annoying consistency.

This approach doesn't work. Men serving time in the friend zone know this approach doesn't work, yet they fall into the same patterns of failure repeatedly because they've been conditioned to place women upon pedestals and hold them in much higher esteem than themselves.

These men don't realise they have low self-esteem, and they're oblivious to how they reveal their low self-esteem to women in their daily social interactions. They're under the false impression they're being respectful while an indeterminable percentage of the women they want to fuck perceive them as simps with no backbones and no balls. Women perceive them as nice guys who do nothing to get their pussies wet, so they toss them into the dreaded friend zone where these poor bastards shall remain.

An indeterminable percentage of decent women see gameless, inexperienced men for the sad simps they are. They see how easily they could exploit them for their attention, money, and time, and bleed them dry, but they decline those ripe opportunities. These women aren't greedy, manipulative, selfish bitches. They're decent, sexually active women with good character. An indeterminable percentage of these women exist, contrary to popular belief, and they spare clueless simps by telling them they're not interested.

An indeterminable percentage of other women, however, lack this decency. Greedy, manipulative, selfish bitches see these men as sad simps too, but they dig their fangs and talons into them, drain them for all of the attention, money, and time they can, and dump them like trash when they've bled them dry to find more fresh simps they can deceive, play with, and cash in on.

When you put yourself and your happiness second to the women you want to fuck, you assure them their value is higher than yours. If you lack the game to recognise this, you don't understand how women don't want to have casual sex with their equals. Women aren't going to do the super freaky, XXX-rated shit to the men they classify as sexually inferior or equal to themselves.

Full-dog alpha males, ladies' men, macks, players, and womanisers fuck comely women, come in their mouths, and the ladies smile and swallow. How are they able to do this consistently? The answer is simple. Women see them as sexually superior men, and they defer accordingly. If women see you as an equal, they see you as a friend, which means you have zero value in their sexual marketplaces.

You probably won't ever get the pussy if this is the case, and this is why you shouldn't put women upon pedestals. This is why you shouldn't place the happiness of women above your own. I tell you this because the men who women truly lust after and want to fuck the most never place the happiness of women above their own.

Full-dog alpha males, ladies' men, macks, players, pimps, and womanisers don't put themselves and their happiness second to women, and they would laugh in your face if you ever suggested something so asinine to them. They know one of the reasons women adore them is because they're so self-centred.

Full-dog alpha males, ladies' men, macks, pimps, players, and womanisers, always put themselves first, they assume the superior position in their sexual dealings with women right from the beginning, and women cooperate with them to the fullest extent. Never put women up on pedestals and never place their happiness above your own because none of that goofy shit will stop them from flaking on you and never talking to you again when their feelings change, and they decide they don't like you anymore.

Don't be another gullible fucking dumb-ass who puts himself second in fruitless attempts to win approval and sexual favour from beautiful women. Don't be afraid to step to comely women with confidence and charm, and tell them what you want from them. If you don't know how to do this, or if you lack the confidence to approach comely women in a bold, straightforward fashion, that's okay. Keep reading. That's why we're here.

Follow my blog at **westcoastwriter.com** and see what you can learn from the game being shared. Buy my books. Read them, apply the information, and follow the steps until tight game becomes your first thought and second language every time you flirt with beautiful women. If you're really having a tough time, email me at **dk@westcoastwriter.com** for a private consultation.

Back to the second date. You went out with Miss Comely last Friday night. She didn't give you the pussy on the first go-round, but she said she wanted to see you again, so you set up a second date. Your pre-date protocol remains the same. Maintain zero contact until Thursday night, and send one text to confirm the date. Don't call her. If Miss Comely doesn't call or text you back Thursday night, that's a red flag.

If she doesn't call or text you by 1700 Friday evening, assume she flaked on you. Abort the date, and launch a new campaign to go fuck some new beautiful women. Don't call or text Miss

Comely. She flaked on you, so she owes you an explanation. Not the other way around. Don't trip if she never calls or texts you again. Charge her to the game, and focus on fucking new beautiful women.

If she calls or texts you back to confirm, your second date is still on. Make sure your place is clean enough for her to fuck you. Make sure your ensemble and grooming are presentable and geared for seduction.

Get sexual with your conversation early on the second date. If she wants you sexually, she's going to get turned on because you let her know it's okay to talk about sex. She's going to feel more comfortable. If she acts offended and uncooperative, kill any thoughts of a third date.

I recommend you spend no more than $25.00 to $35.00 on the first date for two reasons. One, the majority of the women you take on first dates are going to flake on you for the second date, and you're never going to see them again. Two, I have no idea what your dating budget is. There are millions of people reading this book, and I have no idea what their levels of disposable income are.

If you're a sales representative at a credit repair company making $14.00 an hour, and you bring home between $1,100.00 and $1,500.00 biweekly, paying $25.00 to $35.00 on first dates won't do too much damage to your finances. Dating is cool. Dating is fun. Dating is also a luxury. Don't waste money you can't afford to spend trying to impress women who probably never had any real intentions on fucking you anyway.

If you're in the professional-managerial class, you're not a sales representative in a credit repair company taking eight-hour shifts of verbal abuse for minimum wage. If you're in the professional-managerial class, you're an accountant, attorney, doctor, educator, engineer, or financial advisor with upper-middle-class status and a six-figure salary.

Men in that class can easily afford to spend $100.00 to $250.00 on the first date, but that doesn't mean they should. You might be an accomplished accountant, doctor, engineer, or lawyer, however, don't ever make the mistake of thinking your high salary and socially stratified position will stop women from flaking on you if there's a full-dog alpha male, ladies' man, mack, player, or womaniser they would rather suck and fuck.

An indeterminable percentage of women perceive upper-class-men with money and no game as simps too, but they marry them because they're easily controlled, and their generational wealth will keep those women and their offspring in affluence.

To be perfectly curt, women want wealthy simps to provide economic stability and help raise children, but an indeterminable percentage of these financial alpha males still find themselves in second-class positions sexually because their girlfriends, fiancées, and wives cheat on them with and occasionally become impregnated by full-dog alpha males, ladies' men, macks, players, and womanisers.

An indeterminable percentage of the world's women simply can't resist the men whose magnetic masculinity and raw sex appeal turns them on and gets their pussies wet. How you start with women is how you finish. Don't do anything for women from the first hook up or date that you're not willing to keep doing while you're dealing with them. This includes spending money. If you're a lower-income man who makes $20.00 an hour or less, spend no more than $75.00 to $85.00 on the second date.

Miss Comely can flake on you at a moment's notice, so watch how much energy, money, and time you invest in her. You're not here to treat women like queens. Not unless you're the crown prince and male heir apparent to the throne of an imperial or royal monarchy. If you're not a crown prince, treating women you barely know like queens is some stupid ass simp shit. You're not here to treat women you want to fuck like queens either.

You want to see if women are cool, fun, and if you can fuck them in every hole. This is true for the men in the professional-managerial class as well. You have higher social status and more money than your lower-income brethren and women are attracted to that, but, how you start in a hook up or date is how you're going to finish too. Your money and social class won't change the game.

Don't do anything for women from the first hook up or date you're not willing to maintain while you're dealing with them. You have more disposable income to spend on dates, but you're not here to throw your money away on women you're never going to fuck, are you?

Spend no more than $100.00 to $250.00 on the second date. Miss Comely can flake on you, your high salary, your family wealth, your advanced degrees, and your high social status at a moment's notice, so watch how much energy, money, and time you invest in women.

Full-dog alpha males, ladies' men, macks, players, and womanisers don't worry about this because they don't take women on dates. They barely spend money on women. Women crave stiff dick, erotic dirty talk, and hardcore XXX-rated sex from full-dog alpha males, ladies' men, macks, players, and womanisers so much they will flake on you to go fuck them. Consider this when you're trying to figure out how much to spend on a second date.

2 APR 18 (MON)
1241/The Valley
Mission Hills, Los Angeles, California

CHAPTER 17

Third Date

Miss Comely returned your text on Thursday night, confirmed the second date, and asked if you wanted to go paintballing. You had no interest in paintballing because you already had an evening planned at Pacific Park on Santa Monica Pier and Arclight Hollywood.

Miss Comely texted she loved Pacific Park and asked if you've ever gone paintballing before. You texted no. She asked you to give it a try, promised she would make it worth your time, and bid you goodnight before you could protest further.

You didn't want to go paintballing. You wanted to fuck her though, and the prospect of paintballing became more intriguing the longer you considered it. You were smoking blunts at work Friday morning when you received a lengthy text. She sent you a checklist for first time paintballers and advised you to bring the following:

- A hoodie and dark loose sweatpants you don't mind getting dirty.
- A pair of boots you don't mind getting dirty.
- A pair of fingerless weight lifting gloves.
- A doo rag, hat or headwear of some sort.
- Lots of drinking water.

- A garbage bag to put your dirty clothes in after the game is over.
- A clean outfit for the ride home.
- Old towels to clean off equipment and old hits.

You had another fucked up week at work where you and your lazy ass boss had another falling out, so paintballing seemed like a good way to break work-related stress and tension. You let Miss Comely know you had everything on the checklist, and she sent you the address to Hollywood Sports Paintball And Airsoft Park in Bellflower. Your pig of a boss yelled at you to get off your mobile and get back to work. You entertained lingering thoughts about shooting him in his fat fucking face at point-blank range with a paintball gun.

You left work early, deposited your weekly paycheque at an ATM, went home, and got dressed for paintball. You rolled three blunts of Abusive OG and smoked one on the drive to Bellflower. There were clear blue skies above with no cops in sight. You pulled up on Miss Comely in the parking lot where she had paintball guns and mega ammunition. She kissed you hello and thanked you for coming.

You reminded her how she promised to make this worth your time. She laughed and introduced you to the other players. You were cordial during the meet and greet, you caught sour looks from a couple of guys, and you wondered if they fucked Miss Comely in the past. You wondered if they were fuck buddies now. You thought about loading your paintgun and shooting them in their faces at point-blank range.

The introductions ended, and Miss Comely showed you how to load your weapon. You were glad you wore some old cargo pants, and you took all of the extra rounds you could carry. She paid your way into the park and gave you a quick rundown of the rules to capture the flag. She gave you another kiss, and the match began.

You never went paintballing before, so you had no idea you would enjoy shooting at other human beings quite so much. On a scale of one to ten, playing capture the flag with Miss Comely was a solid eight-point-five in terms of enjoyment. You drove home to shower and dress for your date and smoked the second blunt on the way back.

Dusk. You met Miss Comely on the Santa Monica Pier where you ate and hung out at Pacific Park for an hour or so. She loved the Ferris wheel. You took her to see a movie at the ArcLight. She wanted to grab a drink after the flick, so you stopped at this cosy little neighbourhood bar near your place. You were ready to pay for the first round, but she asked you to put your credit card back in your wallet.

You started making out with her after the third round, and you invited her back to your place after the fourth round. She accepted your invitation, paid the bar tab after the sixth round, and you took her back to the crib.

You poured two Booty Claps on the rocks and lit the third blunt. The cocktails and cannabis led to more making out on your couch, which carried over to your bed. You got her butt ass naked. Her deepthroat swallowed you whole, almost made you come. It took all of your willpower to not bust a nut. You couldn't wait to fuck this sexy ass bitch. You waited all week for this moment!

You slid a condom on, threw her legs all the way back so you could go balls deep up in the pussy, then she said things were moving too fast. She slipped her thong on, grabbed her bra and left your bedroom.

You tried to talk her back into bed to no avail. She snatched her clothes up from your sofa and got dressed. She put her flats on, gave you a kiss in parting, and left you perplexed with a rock-hard dick.

This happened to one of my clients. He sent an email at **dk@ westcoastwriter.com**, asked what he did wrong, and whether he should charge his fuck interest to the game. Let's refer to his fuck interest as Miss Blue Balls. He also sent a generous donation which guaranteed his inquiry would be answered within twenty-four hours, so I was happy to earn my money and help him out.

Let's tackle the first question. What did he do wrong? This isn't a matter of right and wrong because there was no clear violation of the game here. My client got Miss Blue Balls naked in his bed, so it's clear he did something right.

However, he also did something and/or said something which made her hesitate to have casual sex with him and he had to accept his responsibility for that. His ego was bruised because he showed Miss Blue Balls a good time, spent money, got her butt ass naked in his bed, he thought he was about to make it happen, but she didn't have casual sex with him.

Men go through bullshit like this every day. It is neither special nor unique. I showed my client how to put his emotions aside, analyse the sexual rejection logically so he could observe the game, and learn from the experience. He learned how to look beyond his hurt feelings, observe how women categorise men, based upon their wants and needs, and adjust his game accordingly.

Let's rephrase the question. Why didn't Miss Blue Balls have casual sex with my client on their second date? The answer is obvious. She wants more than casual sex from him. Women have different designs and purposes for different men, and she decided he has the potential to be more than the next fuck buddy in her life. Whether this is true or not remains to be seen, but that's what she thinks, and she got that idea from something he did or said on one of their dates.

Men and women classify each other and put each other in different, little boxes based upon sex appeal. This isn't fair, this isn't nice, but this is real, and this is how human beings and sexual attraction works on Earth. It is what it is. An indeterminable percentage of men, which certainly appears to be the majority, tend to place women into one of two boxes: fuckable and unfuckable.

An indeterminable percentage of women, which certainly feels like the majority, tend to place men into one of three boxes: boyfriend material, fuck buddy, and unfuckable. The unfuckables are self-explanatory. Women don't fuck those men, but they keep them close enough to use them for attention, emotional support, and money whenever the need arises.

Women have the kinkiest casual sex with their fuck buddies who tend to be full-dog alpha males, ladies' men, macks, players, and womanisers. Women love fucking these men for the sheer, carnal pleasure of having sex. Women lust after these men, so they don't make them wait for sex, and they don't ask them to enter into short-term or long-term monogamous relationships either.

Women make no such demands because they see no futures for themselves with their fuck buddies. This is a fantasy come true until the fuck buddy wants to be monogamous, and his true love rejects him and breaks his heart because he's not boyfriend material. The realisation that he's a sex toy in the eyes of the beautiful woman he desires most finally dawns upon the full-dog alpha male. That's a tough pill to swallow.

The men who represent boyfriend material might be high-quality husband material. High-quality father material. High-quality life partner material. These men represent the future and worlds of possibilities to the indeterminable percentage of women who want long-term monogamous relationships, marriage, children, grandchildren, great-grandchildren, and domestic bliss as we know it. Millions of single women in America and millions more in industrialised countries around the world are looking for single men with highly coveted boyfriend material.

Once a woman classifies you as boyfriend material, two things happen. First, she gets excited and drops you in her boyfriend material box. Second, she starts investing in building her future with you as your next girlfriend.

She didn't put you in her fuck buddy box, so she isn't interested in having casual sex with you. She's interested in becoming your girlfriend, she doesn't want to be the next piece of pussy you fuck and forget about, and these desires will influence her sexual behaviour when she's with you.

A woman can have casual sex with a fuck buddy on the first day they met and justify it on the grounds it was fun, she was horny, and she has no future plans for the fuckboy. He was something fun to do at the time, but she wouldn't want him to be her boyfriend even if he volunteered to fill the position. She classified him as a fuck buddy and put him in the appropriate box where he shall remain.

The same woman who handed her fuck buddy the pussy at the drop of a hat won't fuck the man she classified as boyfriend material on the first or second date. We already know this woman is a promiscuous fucking slut with little to no sexual inhibitions, so why is she making Mr. Boyfriend Material wait for sex?

She's making Mr. Boyfriend Material wait because she wants to hold on to him for the future. He might seem cool, but she knows nine times out of ten he's going to think she's a slut or a whore if she has casual sex with him too soon. She wanted to suck Mr. Boyfriend Material's dick and fuck him the first day she met him. Make no mistake about this. Perceive the game, human nature, and human sexuality for what they truly are.

Mr. Boyfriend Material got her wet, but she's wary because another guy she liked dumped her two weeks ago. She thought he was boyfriend material too. She liked him so much she gave him anal, oral, and vaginal sex on the first hook up.

She went full AOV, and he stopped calling and texting her. He came all over her face like a porn star and dropped her like a bad habit. His abrupt rejection and her dashed hopes cut her deeply and left her damaged, so she's determined not to make the same mistake twice.

She wants to be taken seriously as a potential girlfriend. She doesn't want Mr. Boyfriend Material to perceive her as a slut or a whore. She wants casual sex with a man to lead to a hot, romantic, long-term monogamous relationship for once in her life.

She doesn't want to stop going on dates. She doesn't want to stop enjoying the time and attention of a man she really likes. Experience has shown her this will stop if she has casual sex too soon, so she pretends she doesn't want to fuck. She pretends she wants to take things slow.

This is complete bullshit, but she wants Mr. Boyfriend Material to be her man, so she doesn't go back to his place on the first date. She certainly wants to, but she knows if she goes back to his place she's going to smoke some weed, have a couple of nightcaps, and fuck his fucking brains out. She might go full AOV, but she got dumped the last time she did that, so she declines his invitation and gives him a goodnight kiss instead.

She doesn't have casual sex with him on the second date either. She wants to fuck him even more now because the sexual tension is enormous, but she keeps her eyes focussed on the big picture. She keeps her sexual desires at bay to protect the future she wants to build with this man. She becomes the illusion Mr. Boyfriend Material needs to believe in so he can happily make her his new girlfriend.

This is how an indeterminable percentage of the world's female population become girlfriends and wives. They lie, conceal their true sexual natures, and turn themselves into fuckable illusions men can fall in love with. This isn't fair, this isn't nice, but this is real, and this is how human beings and sexual attraction works on Earth. It is what it is.

Let's get back to my client and Miss Blue Balls. She put him in her boyfriend material box. This should be crystal clear by now. This is why she went on two dates without fucking him yet. If you've ever been on two dates with a woman without fucking her, either she's using you for attention and free food and drink, or she dropped you in her boyfriend material box. The same game that I gave my client applies to you as well.

Women are slick. Observe how Miss Blue Balls assumed control of the situation. She stonewalled my client for sex, told him things were moving too fast (which was bullshit), classified him as boyfriend material, and he doesn't even know if he's the only man in that box or not. There's a chance my client could be the only man in her boyfriend material box, and there's also a chance I could be the Prince of Wales and heir apparent to the British throne with a residence at Clarence House.

It's much more likely my client and three or four other guys, are rolling around in her boyfriend box. Like unsharpened, yellow No. 2 pencils. She will select the man she likes best when she's ready, and focus her attention, resources, and time on him. This is the game Miss Blue Balls is running on my client, and she's winning. With that said, fuck her game. I taught my client how to play a game he could win, and you can do the same.

Question #1 — How did my client end up in this situation? What did he do wrong?

Answer — That's hard to say. He might not have done anything wrong. He can't control which box a woman puts him in, and neither can you. Women are going to place you in the box which works best for them.

Men have no control over how women perceive them and size them up. That's out of their hands, but men have complete control over how direct and straightforward they are about casual sex whenever they meet beautiful women they want to fuck. Don't be shy. Don't be scared. I encouraged my client to be direct with the women he wants to fuck, and I'm giving you the same advice.

My client took Miss Blue Balls on two cool dates. He spent a lot of time and attention with her, and an indeterminable percentage of women enjoy men's nonsexual companionship just as much if not more than sexual intercourse. He never considered this until I brought it to his attention, but once Miss Blue Balls saw she could have fun with him with her clothes on, she might have started seeing him as an awesome boyfriend. My client might have put himself in her boyfriend material box, actually, and you want to learn from his oversight.

Question #2 — Should he charge Miss Blue Balls to the game?

Answer — No. She hasn't done anything wrong. Yet. She's guarding her position and playing good defence, which is what every smart player does in the game. She got butt ass naked in my client's bed. She let him see, smell, and taste her body so he wouldn't be able to stop thinking about her until he sees her again. An indeterminable percentage of sexually active women are slicker than oil, homie. They know how to work us.

Miss Blue Balls let him kiss, lick, smell, and touch the pussy, but she didn't let him fuck the pussy. She gave him head-phones, and he almost came. She gave him a taste of her oral sex potential and fucked his head up. She can probably suck every drop of semen out of a man's balls and leave him flat on his back like a flipped tortoise.

She also took my client paintballing and paid his way into the park. She spent money on the second date of her own volition. I see no reason to charge her to the game. Yet. Don't grow cross with a woman just because her game is tighter than yours. Make a power move and change the game.

Let's get back to Miss Comely.

The third date is at your place. Keep it simple. Dinner, Netflix, cannabis, strong drinks, and lots of kissing and touching. The third date needs to be intimate from start to finish. You're inviting Miss Comely over to fuck you. Take her to the grocery store and buy the night's food and drink together. Go to the dispensary and buy the weed together. Go back to the crib and cook dinner together. Eat. Drink. Watch Netflix. Smoke weed. Laugh. Drink some more. Laugh. Make out. Fuck.

Keep the third date simple because this is where the rubber meets the road. If Miss Comely stops playing games and has casual sex with you, you can keep dealing with her. If you wish. I recommend you approach more beautiful women and meet some fine ass freaks who won't play silly games when it's time to get naked and fuck. If she declines to have sex with you for the third time, charge her to the game.

You don't have half a second to waste on women who don't cooperate with you sexually. Women know whether they want to fuck men or not seconds to minutes after they first meet. They don't need to go out with you on three dates to make a decision they made on the day they met you. Does this make sense?

You're not here to date women and share your energy, money, and time with them if they aren't feeding you, fucking you, and sharing their money with you. You're not here to let any of these women waste your time.

Don't let deceitful women offer flimsy excuses as to why they don't want to fuck you. Don't entertain one word from the lips of women who refuse to cooperate with you sexually because there's nothing to talk about. Cut the bullshit short, tell them to gather their belongings, and have a good night.

Charge all uncooperative pretenders to the game, delete their contact information from your mobile, and don't contact them again. If any of these women call or text you, it's your judgment call if you want to deal with them or not. Experience has taught me not to fuck with such feather-headed, flighty women at all. Follow this protocol with every woman who refuses to have casual sex with you by the third date.

8 APR 18 (SUN)
2154/The Valley
Mission Hills, Los Angeles, California

CHAPTER 18

No Simping After You Get The Pussy

An indeterminable percentage of heterosexual teenage males and men have a prevailing attraction to and innate weakness for physically beautiful women. Therefore, an indeterminable percentage of fiancées, girlfriends, and wives feel insecure and intimidated when physically beautiful women are around them and their men. These women of common beauty know they can't compete.

They know their lovers will betray their trust, cheat on them, and quite possibly leave them for physically beautiful women. The average American heterosexual male gets wobbly for a comely woman, and his frailty increases a hundredfold if he fucks her. There's no room for weakness in the game if you want to have casual sex with multiple beautiful women, and there's no simping after you get the pussy.

Let's say you're just looking to hook up with a woman for casual sex. Take her to a bar to grab a drink or three, and go back to your place or hotel/motel room to fuck. If she doesn't cooperate, charge her to the game.

You have no reason to call or text women who don't give you one hundred percent cooperation sexually. If you feel any hesitancy at deleting their contact information from your mobile, recognise your unwillingness as the deeply ingrained, subconscious simp within you desperately clinging to a shred of hope casual sex might happen later.

Fuck that. Fuck later. Charge uncooperative women to the game. Kill the ingrained, subconscious simp deep within. It's not going to happen overnight. It's a process. It will take time for you to unlearn your simp behaviour, but the journey of ten thousand miles begins with the first step.

Your odyssey in the game begins with learning how to read women quickly and correctly, recognising when they have low to no interest in you sexually, and charging them to the game as soon as possible, so you don't waste precious time.

Let's say the woman cooperated fully and fucked you on the first hook up. Congratulations. The only pleasure sweeter than getting revenge or finding golden treasure is having wild, unprotected sex with comely women. Bust nuts all over her face porn star style. Give her some pearls. It's all part of the experience so enjoy yourself to the fullest, but there's no simping after you get the pussy.

The only time you text women is to set up dates and hook up for casual sex. You've already established this pattern of communication, and there's absolutely no reason to change it. Don't call or text women if you're not fucking them. Don't call just to say hello. Don't send good morning and good night texts. Don't let your clingy, needy, simp energy get the best of you, and strangle the sexual attraction your fuck buddies have for you.

Don't treat these women any differently than the fuck buddies they are. Women have sex with you because they want to climax and come. They aren't doing you any favours when they fuck you. Get that straight in your mind. If you think otherwise, you have another subconscious, simp sensibility you need to change. Women aren't doing you any favours when they have casual sex with you, so there's no simping after you get the pussy.

Maybe you're looking for a serious relationship with a long-term monogamous girlfriend or a long-term girlfriend in an open relationship. Use the three-date closing strategy. You already know how much to spend on the first and second dates. If the woman you're interested in hasn't fucked you by the second date, invite her over to your place for the third date.

If she still refuses to have casual sex with you, invite her to leave your home, and charge her to the game. You've been on three dates with a woman who knew whether she was going to have casual sex with you or not when you first met her. You're not here to take women out on dates, share your attention, energy, money, and time with them and not fuck them.

Women aren't obligated to have sex with you. I want to make this crystal clear. Women aren't obligated to have sex with you, and they don't owe you anything just because you took them out on a date. Women don't owe you shit.

You don't owe women jack shit either. At all. An indeterminable percentage of deceitful, manipulative women will attempt to make you feel otherwise, but you aren't obligated to share any of your attention, energy, money, and time with them. That's why you're going to charge uncooperative women to the game if they don't fuck you by the third date.

Let's say she cooperates and has sex with you on the third date. Congratulations. You might have fucked your future girlfriend, and that's awesome, but there's no simping after you get the pussy. Don't treat her any differently.

Her sex might have been the best you've had in a while. That's cool. Her pussy might have been deeper than the Mariana Trench and tighter than a new keyhole. You want some more of that, right? I thought so. Observe the wisdom of the game and follow it accordingly. There is absolutely no simping after you get the pussy.

10 APR 18 (TUE)
2240/The Valley
Mission Hills, Los Angeles, California

CHAPTER 19

If You Never Hear From Her Again

Remember Betty Bubble Ass? It was Friday evening, and you were at the Red Line Hollywood/Highland station waiting for the train to North Hollywood when you saw Betty coming down the stairs. The platform was full, but you cut through the crowd and caught up to her just as the train arrived.

You and Betty stepped into the subway car and were sardines packed in a tin. You took immediate advantage of the close quarters with her breasts pressed into your arm and spit straightforward game about hooking up for casual sex with a splash of dirty talk. She blushed, smiled, and gave you her new number.

You followed proper hook up protocol and took her to a bar about ten minutes away from your place where you had a couple of drinks, smoked a blunt outside, had some more drinks, did a few lines in the men's room, then you took Betty back to the crib where you fucked her to sleep. She woke up the next morning, served you breakfast in bed, watched some of the Lakers-Clippers game with you, fucked you at halftime, and left.

Betty was a nine, easily the finest woman you fucked in the last few weeks, and you couldn't believe how easy it was. You urged all of your friends to buy my book. You became a born again believer in the game. You hooked up with Betty again and again and again. And again. Then you texted her one Friday evening, and she didn't text you back. You waited a couple of days, texted her again, and received no response. You called her, and she didn't answer. It's been two weeks since you heard from her, and you're wondering what happened.

Betty has somebody. That's what happened.

That's why you haven't heard from her. He could be a short-term boyfriend, long-term boyfriend, baby daddy, short-term fiancé, forever fiancé, or husband. Or, she could have a woman who's her short-term girlfriend, long-term girlfriend, short-term fiancée, forever fiancée, or wife. People get down all kinds of ways these days.

The ugly truth is Betty has a man (or a woman), and she's not going to leave him (or her) for you. You're probably never going to fuck that bubble ass again. Accept the reality of the situation, charge her to the game, and launch a new campaign for casual sex with more beautiful women.

Don't call or text her anymore. Don't simp for her or other women who stop calling you, and drop out of your life because the time came for them to return to their true lovers. Accept the reality of the situation, charge her to the game, and mount a new campaign for casual sex with more beautiful women.

Rookie: That's fucked up, Dennis.

Dennis: It is what it is. Everything is fair in the game, homie.

Rookie: I know, but that was some bullshit, my nigga. Her pussy was so good.

Dennis: Indeed. She put it on you. That's why you can't stop thinking about her.

Rookie: That bubble ass is all in my head, man! Why she let me hit in the first place?

Dennis: Betty Bubble Ass and her true lover fell out. We don't know what happened, and we won't speculate, but she stepped out of her relationship to fuck around for a minute and met you. You gamed her up and made her feel good about herself. You gave her self-esteem a positive boost, and she rewarded you with the pussy. That's all it was.

Rookie: No, nigga. See, you went to college, you wrote a book, and you think you know some shit. You don't understand, my nigga. It was deeper than that. Why she let me hit multiple times?

Dennis: I've been through this silly shit multiple times, and you're thinking way too much about a female you should charge to the game because it's over. Betty fucked you till she had her fill because you hit her pussy with the magic wand. You made the bitch come buckets.

She liked the way you fucked her so much she came back for seconds, thirds, fourths and fifths. She had her little fun with you for a season, but she went back to the lover she truly cares for when all was said and done. You were her plaything for a minute. That's all it was. She doesn't love you, and she might not even like you truth be told, lil' homie.

Don't call, email, or text women after they ghost you. Maintain zero contact permanently. Never debase yourself and grovel at the fucking feet of any of these fucking women for some fucking pussy. Begging should be beneath you.

If you fucked a woman so well where it was hard to breathe because she squeezed your core with her thighs from coming multiple times, and she ghosted you right out of the blue, recognise the situation for what it is, understand she has a true lover she cares for more than you, and charge her to the game. Go meet some new beautiful women, step to them the same way, and continue your casual campaign to fuck the shit out of them.

You have nothing to feel bad about. You wanted to fuck Betty Bubble Ass, and you did that. You fucked her, but you never captured her heart. Her pussy was so good, and she was so comely, you grew attached and developed feelings for her. You got caught up in the wild lust of raw sex, developed a moderate case of the feels, and this is understandable because you're a rookie. You haven't learned how to cut the cord between your heart and your dick when you fuck women.

If you want to become a master at having casual sex with multiple comely women, you can't grow attached to any of them. You can't open your heart to the women you fuck. You can't fall in love. The game is glacial. Predatory. It isn't for everyone who thinks they want to play. You have to be emotionally unavailable, icy, and selfish if you want to master the game of getting women for casual sex.

12 APR 18 (THU)
0008/Canter's Deli
Fairfax District, Los Angeles, California

CHAPTER 20

A Word About PT

It's no secret that the indeterminable segment of the global female population who are sexually attracted to fit, muscular men with lots of money certainly appears to be the majority. I knew this at an early age, so I find it safe to assume that an indeterminable percentage of teenagers and young adults in the U.S. and other industrialised countries know this as well. This doesn't sound like a topic which requires in-depth academic research, does it?

I wanted to see what other people across the Earth's surface thought about this, so I went to Google, typed in women are attracted to men with muscles, and websites from askmen. com, theguardian.com, independent.co.uk, menfitness.com, newsweek.com, and washingtonpost.com appeared on the first page of the search engine's results.

All of the different articles reached the same conclusion: women and gay men are more attracted to muscular, powerful, rich men because they lust after power, strength, and wealth. I didn't need an anthropologist, a study from a university, or a website from the first page of a Google search to tell me this and neither do you. Let's return to the money, looks and status argument which is frailer than my infirm ninety-year-old grandfather way down south in Muscle Shoals, Alabama.

I find the looks, money, and status argument insubstantial because it's invalid, and an indeterminable segment of the Earth's male population twists this invalid argument to make excuses for their failure to have casual sex with beautiful women which is weak as fuck. A man will never develop and grow either in the game or in wisdom by defending his sexual insecurities and making excuses for his shortcomings. That behaviour is weak as fuck.

Perhaps you were born into power, privilege, and wealth in the elite classes of society. Perhaps you were born a few rungs down on the socioeconomic ladder into a solid upper-middle-class family. You're not rich by any means, but you're not struggling either. Perhaps you were born into the impoverished masses of poor, ignorant, unhappy bastards scraping the bottom.

You had no control over that. Which is much better for the world, such as it is, because if people could choose their parents, the poor would remain perpetually childless. Lack of wealth, however, doesn't stop an indeterminable percentage of poor full-dog alpha males, ladies' men, macks, players, and womanisers from fucking an indeterminable percentage of rich, beautiful women. Don't blame your lack of financial wealth for your failure to have casual sex with the women you desire.

Perhaps you don't have high status in society. It's exceedingly difficult to attain high status in a capitalist economic system if you don't own the means of production and lack financial wealth, but this obstacle doesn't stop an indeterminable percentage of poor men from fucking beautiful, upper-class women in every hole. Don't blame your level of status in society for your failure to have casual sex with the women you desire.

Perhaps you weren't blessed with an attractive, symmetrical face and fine features. You had no control over how your face was shaped according to your genetic code. Women universally prefer handsome men, but their preference doesn't stop an indeterminable percentage of men without attractive, symmetrical faces from fucking an indeterminable percentage of beautiful women. Don't blame your looks for your failure to have casual sex with the women you desire.

What you do have control over is your ability to work out, increase your flexibility, muscle mass, and stamina, and become the most physically fit man you were born to become. You can do this. No one can stop you from doing this but you, and you're the most obstinate foe you will ever face in your struggles for self-improvement.

Women have always been sexually attracted to muscular men because they're drawn to their power and raw physicality. This is particularly true when women decide to engage in casual sex. An indeterminable percentage of men refuse to believe women can have casual sex without forming emotional connections with their partner(s) either before or after the fucking. I have to step in and separate the game from the truth for these deeply deluded men.

An indeterminable percentage of women have casual sex with men they have no emotional connections with. An indeterminable percentage of women have casual sex with men they don't want to form futures with. An indeterminable percentage of women have casual sex in the same cavalier fashion men do. These are ugly, uncomfortable truths an indeterminable percentage of men cannot accept.

When women are cruising for casual sex, they want to fuck their fantasies and enjoy all sorts of debauchery with no strings attached. When women are prowling for mates, their selection criteria changes significantly. It's not all about lust and carnality anymore. A man's level of education comes to the fore. Does he have a bachelor's degree? A master's degree? A PhD? Or is he a high school dropout?

A high school dropout with long hair, broad shoulders, massive biceps, pecs, triceps, washboard abs, and tattoos might be an awesome, mind-blowing fuck for a season. But that same man might not make the best husband and father for a driven, career woman in corporate America with advanced degrees because his low level of education will hamper his future earning potential.

The sexiest men who fuck multiple women with the greatest prowess don't normally make good husbands, fathers, and life partners. Full-dog alpha males, ladies' men, macks, players, and womanisers are here for a good time. Not a long time. It is what it is, and the majority of women from different ethnic groups appear to understand this part of the game.

Black American women are a notable and rather embarrassing exception because an indeterminable percentage of them, which certainly appears to be the majority, regard college-educated black American men as educated lames and shun them either for black American men with less formal education, or non-black men with college degrees. The hypocrisy these game goofy, idiot ass black American females practise is bottomless, but I digress...

When women are hunting for husbands, a man's finances becomes a source of concern. Does he command a six-figure salary? Is he a millionaire? Is he a billionaire? Does he collect minimum wage paycheques bi-weekly? Is he unemployed?

The potential husband's social class becomes a source of concern depending on the woman's socioeconomic background and what she expects him to provide for her and her future child(ren). Does he come from a wealthy family? An upper middle-class family? A blue-collar, working-class family? Is his family below the poverty line?

Women still adore muscles and good looks. They're a constant source of sexual attraction, but there's an indeterminable percentage of women who place much higher priorities on men's levels of education, social status, and wealth when they're looking to marry and create families.

If you want to fuck multiple women through hook ups and dates, I encourage you to exercise and engage in regular physical training. You can lift weights. You can do calisthenics. You can swim. You can train at a boxing gym. You can buy a bike, and start riding to develop the legs and lungs of a cyclist. You can do all of these things and more.

Pick the physical activities which motivate you to get up off of your ass and out of your home three to four times a week. Regular physical training will help you become your best physical self, and it could help you live longer. Here are ten benefits you'll enjoy if you follow my advice. Regular physical training:

1. Increases your level of happiness. This is why people feel better after exercising whether it was a mild, moderate, or intense workout.
2. Helps you sleep better.
3. Boosts your energy.
4. Reduces your risk of heart disease.
5. Increases your strength and flexibility.
6. Improves your memory.
7. Increases your self-confidence.
8. Improves productivity and helps you perform better at work.
9. Fortifies your immune system and makes you less susceptible to disease.
10. Helps people live longer.

Take full advantage of the benefits from regular physical training, develop your best masculine self, and do this for yourself first and foremost. An indeterminable percentage of the women you meet will be sexually attracted to your muscular physique, and that's cool. That's the icing on the cake. Use women's adoration and lust to your advantage, but don't let that bullshit go to your head. Talk to enough bodybuilders, and you'll learn women still flake on men even if they have thirty-inch biceps.

Should you join a gym? That's a great question which begs two more. First, do you have the disposable income where you can easily afford a gym membership? Second, do you have the desire and discipline to hit the gym and work out three to four times a week for 52.1429 weeks?

Millions of Americans get gym memberships every January as part of their New Year's resolutions, yet eighty percent of them stop working out within five months. Don't commit yourself financially and just quit. Especially if it's a struggle to pay for it.

If you have the discipline, disposable income, drive, and time to exercise at a gym regularly, get a membership, and start working out. Today. If you don't, then a gym membership might be an extra expense you don't need to add to your monthly budget right now. Joining a gym is a luxury, not a necessity. You don't have to join a gym to exercise regularly.

You can exercise at home. All you need is a floor, and some open space where you can stretch, and do burpees, crunches, leg raises, push-ups, and squats where you use your body weight for resistance. If you live near a park which has monkey bars, parallel bars, pull-up bars, and wall bars all in one location, then you can add back levers, chin-ups, and pull-ups to your calisthenics regimen. Doing calisthenics at home and your local park don't require a monthly or yearly gym membership.

We're all at different points in our lives. Some of us are richer than others, some of us are poorer than others, but every healthy, able-bodied man can exercise, lift weights, or do calisthenics to build muscle and train himself physically. Women are sexually attracted to muscular men. Remember this the next time you want to sit on your ass, roll a blunt, crack a brew, and watch sports when you know you really ought to go the gym and hit the weights, or hit the floor and do one hundred push-ups.

14 APR 18 (SAT)
1505/The Valley
North Hollywood, Los Angeles, California
Happy Birthday, Tori!

CHAPTER 21

Work On Your Game

I told you back in chapter five that hooking up with women and going on dates is a numbers game. If you're serious about learning the game and applying it to your daily life to fuck multiple women, you have to approach a lot more beautiful women than you're probably approaching now. You have to approach women when you're nervous, uncomfortable, and your words are stuck in your throat. I want you to understand this moving forward.

You're going to approach a beautiful woman one day, she's going to smile at you, and you're going to forget everything you were going to say to her. Don't fold like a bad poker hand when this happens. Don't get scared and surrender. Freestyle with the game. Let your charm and natural instincts take over. Don't think about what you're going to say. Smile, lose yourself in the moment, let the player energy flow, and talk your way into the pussy.

You're going to approach these women and get rejected by the bulk of them. Rejection is part of the game, so don't get discouraged. Push past the rejection, keep approaching the beautiful women you want to fuck, keep working on your game every day, and you're going to see results. Practise makes perfect, and your game with women will tighten up.

You'll get rejected less as you become more comfortable approaching women, your confidence will grow, and your delivery will become more authentic, which makes it much more believable. Some of the beautiful women who are sexually attracted to you will cooperate, hook up with you, date you, and you will enjoy the casual sex you seek.

The effort and energy you invest into your game will be reflected in your results. If you want to fuck multiple beautiful women, you have to approach them for casual sex every day. Practise makes perfect.

Michael Jordan knew a thing or two about practise. He also knew a thing or two about pouring effort and energy into his game. He led the Chicago Bulls to six NBA championships and earned six NBA Finals Most Valuable Player honours to go along with the diamond-studded rings and Larry O'Brien trophies.

Jordan knew the immeasurable value of practise and working on his game every day. No player leads an NBA team to six championships and avoids defeat in the NBA Finals without having an elite work ethic second to none, and dedicating himself one hundred percent to winning games.

YouTube has a video of an interview between Michael Jordan and Ahmad Rashad. The dated, grainy video is called "Michael Jordan. How Important Is Practise?" During the interview, Ahmad Rashad talked about how Jordan's teammates told the Chicago press playing against him in practise was like competing in an actual game.

Jordan acknowledged he worked so hard in practise that NBA games became routine to him. What happened in actual games wasn't anything he hadn't seen before in practise. Think about that for a moment. How much basketball do you have to practise until NBA games become routine to you? That shit is insane, but I digress...

"Work ethic eliminates fear," Jordan said. "So if you put forth the work, then what are you fearing? You know what you're capable of doing, and what you're not. I practise as if I'm playing in a game, so when the moment comes in a game, it's not new to me. That's the beauty of the game of basketball. That's the reason why you practise. That's the effort, so when you get to that moment, you don't have to think. Things just instinctively happen."

Jordan's most bitter rivals, the Detroit Pistons, blocked his path to his first NBA championship. The Bulls kept reaching the Eastern Conference Finals, only to get smacked up and beat the fuck down by the Motor City Bad Boys.

Jordan knew he had to elevate his game if he wanted to defeat the Pistons, advance to the NBA Finals, and claim his first championship, so he committed himself to physical training. He adopted an early morning workout plan where he did an intense hour of lifting weights. He avoided heavy lifting and did agility work with light weights and quick reps instead.

Jordan had a full gym in his basement where he did these new early morning workouts before practise. Ron Harper joined him one morning, and the rest of their teammates gradually joined these early morning sessions. When they finished working out, Jordan's chef served breakfast, and the Breakfast Club was born.

The idea was ingenious. Jordan and his teammates forged a bond through training and eating together, which helped them grow closer together as a unit in their bodies, minds, and spirits.

They also built more endurance, mental focus, and strength from the Breakfast Club workouts, which they did all season long. When Jordan entered the first round of the 1991 NBA playoffs after the eighty-two game regular season, he felt just as fresh as he did in the first game of the preseason.

His teammates felt fresh too, and the Chicago Bulls defeated the Pistons in the Eastern Conference Finals, advanced to the NBA Finals, and won the first of their six NBA championships. What's the moral of the story? Practise makes perfect, and outworking your competition takes you over the top.

The effort, energy, and work ethic Jordan poured into his physical training and practises elevated him from being a star player in Chicago to becoming the most dominant professional basketball player on the planet during his reign. His effort, energy, and work ethic distinguished him from all of his competition and made him an unparalleled champion in the history of American professional sports.

He remains the platinum standard and measuring stick for NBA superstars to this day even though he retired in 2003. Millions of kids, teenagers, and adults, young and old, all around the world, buy and wear Air Jordans in reverence of the living legend.

Enough about Jordan. He's good. Let's get back to you. You want to fuck the beautiful women you desire, and it won't happen if you don't invest effort, energy, and work ethic in your game every day.

Professional athletes practise, train, and hone their skills year-round to stay competitive in their respective leagues. Full-dog alpha males, ladies' men, macks, players, and womanisers practise, train, and hone their skills year-round to stay competitive in the game of getting women. You have to do the same if you want to enjoy sexual success with multiple beautiful women.

When it comes to sexual attraction and talking about sex, confident women are more direct in how they communicate with the men they want to fuck. Less confident women tend to be more indirect.

I like pretty women who enjoy casual sex, I don't know too many heterosexual men who don't, but I much prefer direct women because they're confident and upfront. I know exactly who and what I'm dealing with, and their attitude reflects my own. I get straight to the point with no games or misunder-standings involved, and I appreciate women who do the same.

Before I left Michigan to find freedom and fortune as a writer, I ran the streets of Detroit with Billy Love, a charismatic singer and local celebrity and I wrote at the Majestic Café, known more affectionately as the Majestic to its employees and patrons.

Jean-Paul Sartre wrote at the Café de Flore in Paris, France's best-known postwar literary café, and I wrote at the Majestic on 4120 Woodward Avenue in Midtown Detroit. I had an apart-ment in Lafayette Park at the time, but I couldn't focus and write there for reasons I still haven't ascertained. I had a dope ass view of the downtown Detroit skyline and the downtown Windsor, Ontario, Canada skyline from my living room, but the words never came to me.

There was something about the Majestic, however, which shook the words loose in my mind and created a heavy machine gun flow of characters, conflicts, dialogue, plot lines, resolutions, scenes, settings, and subplots which bled from my red Pilot Precise V7 rolling ball pen across page after page after page in yellow legal pads. I wrote a thousand-page manuscript at the Majestic I have yet to publish, but I digress...

I didn't go to the Majestic to pick up women. I went there because I couldn't believe how my creativity took flight at this neighbourhood bar. Something about the energy of the place opened doors and picked locks in my mind. I caught a clear signal there which was so powerful my relationship with writing deepened and grew intimate.

I married the craft the way athletes marry sports. The way gangsters, hustlers, killers, and pimps marry crime. The way wealthy, bloodthirsty white boys mad with power marry war. Writing became the love of my life. Writing became my reason for waking up in the morning. Writing became my everything, and I started meeting women.

I'd be at the bar with legal pad and pen locked in mental intercourse with my manuscript hunting for the right words to give flavour and form to the story in my mind when a woman would stroll up. If I thought she was cute, which meant she was at least a seven or higher in terms of her physical beauty, I allowed her to interrupt my session for a moment.

If she broke my focus and started running her mouth about nothing I had any interest in, I cut in like a new dance partner and asked when she was buying the first round. If I got the impression she copped an attitude and didn't want to buy me a drink, I cut the conversation off and returned to writing.

Remember, I didn't go to the Majestic to get laid. Casual sex wasn't my priority, and I honestly believe my indifference toward women helped me fuck so many of them. I went there to listen to cool new music courtesy of Anthony, who was Detroit's best-dressed bartender at the time.

I went there to drink and numb the stress from working as a material control supervisor at the Daimler Chrysler Warren Stamping Plant. I hated that fucking job despite its high wages and handsome benefits package. I went to the Majestic to smoke weed and write. I put the craft before ass then as now, so I had no problem cutting the ineffective game of narcissistic attention whores off at the knees, and dismissing them before they could waste any more of my time. They didn't take rejection very well.

Conversely, if the beautiful stranger bought the first round without me having to ask, the conversation moved forward. If I liked her style and she had some good weed, we stepped outside to smoke.

More drinks followed, and if she liked doing coke, we stepped into the men's room where we hit some key bumps. One thing led to another, and I took her back to my crib at

Lafayette Towers Apartment 1908 West, where I promptly put her feet on the ceiling.

These sexcapades became regular rendezvous, and it was easy to do because my crib was five minutes away from the Majestic by car. Logistics is the name of the game when you want to take women back to your place or a hotel/motel room for casual sex.

I gave you an example of how women approached me directly. Some readers can relate because they've had similar experiences themselves, but other readers might not be able to relate at all because this has never happened to them in their lives.

The key demographic of men in the U.S. are males between the ages of eighteen to forty-nine. They're the most desirable group for advertisers, businesses, and women alike, yet an indeterminable percentage of these men don't get approached by women. We covered the true nature of women back in chapter three, and I showed you how they hide their true sexual natures behind plastic smiles, well-maintained façades, and a lie or two.

If women never approach you, they have low to no sexual interest in you. Reach out and contact me when you're ready to change this. If you're the type of guy women approach, they have an undetermined level of sexual interest in you which is a good sign, but it's still no guarantee you're going to fuck them. Don't misinterpret a woman's smile or her attention as a sexual guarantee.

A woman approaches you when she has a strong sexual interest in you, and her interest gives you two edges which can make your game sharper than a samurai's katana and cut straight to the point.

First, she's approaching you, and this gives you the power to accept or reject her. She's given you the power from the beginning, so don't get weak and give it back. Never relinquish power. Second, her sexual interest makes it easier to talk to her. She wants to see what you have to say, so make eye contact and tell this horny chick you want to lick her pussy until her legs start shaking.

You might be the type of man that women approach, and that's cool, but you still have to flirt with them verbally and physically. You still have to escalate your flirting to build the sexual tension to a boil. You still have to stimulate their emotions and carnal imaginations.

You still have to stir their lusts and move them into a mental space where they feel comfortable letting go and letting casual sex happen. You still have to make sure you don't say or do anything stupid, which breaks the seductive mood and turns them off. Don't talk yourself out of the pussy. It's an easy mistake to make when you get a little too loose, so keep your game tight. Laughter charms and disarms. Keep your conversation funny and sexual.

Your job is to talk about casual sex, flirt, initiate physical contact, escalate the touching, build sexual tension, and take her back to the crib or your hotel/motel room. Your job is to keep your game tight from hello until you're balls deep up in your new fuck buddy. Learn to read women quickly and correctly when you approach them for casual sex. Make eye contact and get straight to the point.

A woman's body language sets the tone for her words to follow. You won't learn how to read it overnight because it takes time to study women and learn from their mating behaviour. However, once you become proficient at reading women's body language quickly and correctly, you'll know how they're going to respond before they open their mouths to speak. The body betrays the mouth.

Don't waste time once you start talking. Look beautiful women in their eyes and say what you have to say in forty-five seconds to two minutes tops. Don't let fear hold you back. Step to them, make eye contact, say what you have to say, and read their body language while you talk to them.

1. **Did she smile when you started talking to her?** Yes? This is a good sign. If a woman likes you, she's going to smile when you talk to her. It might be a wide beam where you can see all of her pearly whites, or it might be a shy, more subdued grin which conceals her darker passions, but you're going to see some interest reflected in her face. If a woman doesn't smile while you're talking to her, she might not be feeling you.

2. **Did she move closer to you when you started talking?** Yes? Another good sign. She felt comfortable enough to draw closer to you even though you're a stranger. If a woman doesn't move closer to you when you're talking to her, she might not be feeling you. An indeterminable percentage of men who lack game overlook little cues like that. Don't be one of them.

3. **Did she make eye contact with you?** Yes? Excellent. If a woman doesn't make eye contact with you, this could indicate shyness or lack of interest.

4. **Were her arms crossed when you talked to her?** No? She wasn't closed off to your approach. If her arms were open and relaxed, she was receptive to your game. If a woman's arms remain crossed while you talk to her, she might not be feeling you. There's a part of her that's defensive and closed off to you.

5. **Did she touch you while you spoke to her?** Yes? Good sign. Whenever women flirt with me physically, I know I can fuck them. Men with muscular physiques can attest to this. Women touch their muscles because it turns them on sexually.

When a woman slugs me in the arm, this tells me she wants to feel my triceps or my shoulder, and she also wants to see how I respond to her flirting. Women disguise their sexual advances as "playing" when they're out in public, but their physical play deepens once they're in a private space where casual sex can happen.

The playful tapping and touching become kissing, cock sucking, and fucking. Women will find a way to touch you if they like you, and if they want to touch you, best believe they want to fuck you. If a woman doesn't touch you while you speak to her, she might not be feeling you.

6. **Did she laugh while you talked to her?** If not, she might not be feeling you. If she laughed, that was a good sign. When a woman likes you, she's going to be eager to talk with you. She wants to chat, learn more about you, get completely engaged in the conversation, smile, and laugh with you. And it won't be one of those plastic laughs which come off completely fake like low-quality hair weaves on black women, or disingenuous white boys apologising for their latest displays of racist white supremacist behaviour.

It will be genuine mirth which flows from the spirit. If you can make a woman laugh, you can joke your way right into bending her over and fucking the shit out of her too.

22 APR 18 (SUN)
1458/The Valley
Mission Hills, Los Angeles, California

CHAPTER 22

Credit Repair Builds Confidence

Let's get straight to the point. Your game isn't tight if you have a bad, poor, or fair credit score. Men love sex, so we tend to focus our attention and efforts on getting pussy. We focus on how to approach women, what to say to women, how to flirt with women, how to have sex with women, and how to have sex with multiple women; but we don't put nearly as much attention, effort, and focus into investing our money wisely and maintaining good to excellent credit. This is where multitudes of men lose in the game.

Let's assume you're one of the more fortunate men in life who's tall, muscular, and in excellent health. You have a six-figure income, dress well, drive a fancy car, and you have multiple comely women ready and willing to fuck you and suck you off at your beck and text.

You're living the full-dog alpha life men dream of, and this part of your game is watertight. You're able to get pussy on demand through attraction, which is dope, but if you have a bad, poor, or fair credit score, I advise you to humble yourself a bit and recognise your game isn't as tight as you think it is.

Your credit game needs to be just as tight as your sex game, so don't sacrifice one for the sake of the other. Don't max your credit cards out and ignore the bills because your credit score is going to suffer mightily. Businesses judge people based upon their credit scores, unfortunately, and having bad to poor credit has negative influences over different aspects of your every day life from finding a job to finding a place to live. Let's look at the nine most common side effects of bad to poor credit.

1. **Your credit and loan applications may not be approved**. Creditors will accept a certain amount of risk. They have no choice. It's the cost of doing business, but if you have a credit score that's too low, you become too much of a risk for them to do business with you. They don't want to lend to you due to your bad to poor credit, so they will deny you when you apply for a credit card or a loan.
2. **Difficulty buying a car**. If you need a loan to buy a car, the bank is going to check your credit before approving you for the funds. If you have bad to poor credit, the lender can deny you outright or approve you with a much higher interest rate people with good to excellent credit don't have to pay. Higher interest rates lead to higher monthly payments.
3. **Difficulty renting an apartment**. You don't just move into an apartment. Landlords check the credit of potential tenants before approving rental applications, so having bad to poor credit will make it more difficult to rent a house or an apartment. Landlords take full advantage of people with bad to poor credit and charge them much higher security deposits that people with good to excellent credit don't have to pay.
4. **Difficulty starting your own business**. If you come from a rich family or have investors with deep pockets who believe in your vision, this doesn't apply to you. If you don't have someone else's financial backing and you want to start your own business, you're going to need a loan from a bank. A bad to poor credit history will limit the

amount of money the bank feels comfortable loaning to you if they loan you any money at all. A professional business plan and expertly prepared marketing data won't overcome a bad to poor credit score because it makes you too much of a risk for the bank's comfort.

5. **Higher insurance premiums**. Insurance companies run credit checks too. They justify doing so with misleading babble about lower credit scores being linked to higher claims being filed. This is how they justify running credit checks and charging higher premiums to customers with lower credit scores despite the number of claims those people might have actually filed.

6. **Higher interest rates on your credit cards and loans**. Lenders use your credit score as an indicator of the chances you'll default on a credit card or loan debt. Lenders look at people with bad to poor credit scores as riskier borrowers than those with higher credit ratings. They do business with borrowers who have lower credit scores, but they charge them much higher interest rates. If you're approved for a credit card or a loan with a bad to poor credit score, you're going to pay much more in interest over time.

7. **Required security deposits on utilities.** Utility companies who provide cable, electricity, natural gas, and water check your credit during the application process. Customers with bad to poor credit scores are required to pay a security deposit in order to establish service in their names. Perhaps you've always paid your utility bills on time without fail. That's nice. Utility companies don't give a fuck. If you have bad to poor credit, the security deposit will be charged upfront, and you'll be required to pay it if you want to establish service in your name.

8. **You can't get a cell phone contract**. A cell phone is a necessity these days. A cell phone is a lifeline. Cell phone companies are aware of this, and they run credit checks too. If you have bad to poor credit, they're not going to give you a contract which means you'll have to choose between getting a pre-paid cell phone, a month-to-month contract where phones tend to be more expensive, or you might have to settle for a free Obama phone.

   That's the widely used and misleading nickname of a federal program known as Lifeline which provides cell phone service for millions of low-income subscribers. Having bad to poor credit also means you'll have higher monthly payments than those with good to excellent credit.

9. **You may be denied employment**. You may be denied employment. There are certain jobs which require people to maintain good credit histories. This means applicants are turned down and passed over for promotions due to bankruptcies, excessive debts, and outstanding bills on their credit reports. Accountants, financial professionals, government workers, military members, and some political and security positions require applicants to keep their finances and credit ratings in good standing.

Your credit score holds tremendous sway over nearly every aspect of your life which isn't fair, but this is the way the world works, so you want to repair your credit as soon as possible if it's damaged. Search Google for credit repair companies, do your due diligence, and pick the one which suits you best.

Having good to excellent credit builds your confidence and your financial strength, so repair your credit if that's what you need to do. Lenders are allowed to discriminate against people based upon their credit scores with no questions asked, so protect yourself. Credit repair builds confidence.

Credit Scores:

- Excellent Credit: 750+
- Good Credit: 700-749
- Fair Credit: 650-699
- Poor Credit: 600-649
- Bad Credit: Anything below 600

23 APR 18 (MON)
1230/The Valley
Mission Hills, Los Angeles, California

CHAPTER 23

Avoid Women With Boyfriends, Fiancés, And Husbands

To get weak in the knees is to become helpless with emotion, and an indeterminable percentage of the world's heterosexual male population gets weak in the knees for beautiful women. Some would call this a generalisation. I state this as fact, and I assert this is just as true for the overwhelming majority of the world's heterosexual male population today as it was many millennia ago.

If we look at this historically, the innate, emotional weakness heterosexual men have for beautiful women were major themes in Greek mythology, Roman mythology, and the Holy Bible. This ancient motif has endured the test of time and re-established itself in the comic books, films, graphic novels, novels, screenplays, songs, and stage plays of our age because heterosexual men have the same weaknesses, some things never change, and this is why I encourage you to avoid dealing with women who have boyfriends, fiancés, and husbands.

There is no sex sweeter and more fulfilling to a man's arrogance, ego, and lust than fucking another man's fiancée, girlfriend, or wife and doing every perverted sexual act he can think of to her. There's an indeterminable percentage of men who enjoy dominating other men through fucking their fiancées, girlfriends, and wives.

Make sure you understand the rules before you sit down to play at the black table in the casino of love. Sexual betrayal isn't a sport. It's a risk with potentially lethal consequences. I didn't give half a fuck about those consequences when I was a hot-blooded, reckless, self-destructive fool. I thought differently then. I'm not that man anymore, and I encourage you to cherish life for the priceless gift that it is and avoid dealing with women who have boyfriends, fiancés, and husbands.

I warn you because we have homicidal simps among us. When I think of homicidal simps, the name Elliot Rodger leaps to mind. Rodger unleashed his simpleton savagery on May 23, 2014, in Isla Vista, California, where he murdered six people and wounded fourteen others near the campus of the University of California at Santa Barbara.

His bloody killing spree began when he stabbed three men to death in his apartment. His body count was at three. A narcissistic perpetrator, Rodger wanted the world to know why he found it acceptable to end the lives of others, so he uploaded a video to YouTube, which he called "Elliot Rodger's Retribution."

He was smug enough to outline the details of the killings he planned to commit, and what motivated him to carry out the murders. He said he wanted to punish the women who rejected him sexually and socially and the sexually active men he envied.

Rodger emailed his 107,000-word manifesto, *My Twisted World: The Story of Elliot Rodger* to his therapist, his parents, several family members, and some other acquaintances. He bared his soul to all who read his work where he described his childhood, conflicts within his family, his searing sexual frustration from constant rejection, his inability to get a girlfriend, his hatred of Asian men, black men, women, and interracial couples. He also described what he referred to as his retribution.

Rodger left his apartment and drove to a sorority house where he shot three female students outside. Two of those victims died. Rodger drove to a nearby eatery where he shot and killed a man dining inside. His body count rose to six. He sped through Isla Vista where he shot and wounded seven people and wounded seven more by ramming them with his BMW.

Gunplay with the police followed.

Rodger sustained a non-fatal wound to his hip and crashed into a parked vehicle. Police found him dead in his black Beamer from a self-inflicted gunshot wound to the head, with three 9mm semi-automatic handguns (two SIG Sauer 9226 pistols and one Glock 34 Longslide pistol) and 400 unspent rounds. Rodger's body count rose to seven, and thus ended the life of America's most infamous homicidal simp who subsequently became the patron saint of Inceldom, and inspired an indeterminable percentage of other despondent, mentally ill, racist, sexually frustrated men to follow his black-pill path.

An indeterminable percentage of boyfriends, fiancés, and husbands become homicidal simps after they learn their girlfriends, fiancées, and wives have betrayed them with other men. These men have an overwhelming desire to commit murder, and they feel justified in seeking revenge.

An indeterminable percentage of women lie. Some of them lie every now and then, and some of them lie like they fucking breathe. Deception is part of the game, so when you approach women for casual sex or dating, expect an indeterminable percentage of them to lie about their relationship statuses or conceal the truth altogether and not mention their boyfriends, fiancés, and husbands.

If you discover a woman you're dealing with has a boyfriend, fiancé, or husband, I encourage you to charge her to the game, maintain zero contact and don't reach out to re-establish relations in the future. Charge deceptive girlfriends, disingenuous fiancées, and scheming wives to the game and continue your campaign with single, unattached, childless women.

There are boyfriends, fiancés, and husbands who are so insecure with themselves and their romantic relationships, they have their girlfriends, fiancées, and wives followed, photographed, and filmed by private investigators. You don't want to be the other man in the surveillance video. Trust me on this.

The insecure boyfriend, fiancé, or husband could start following you around with a Glock 19 semi-automatic pistol in his lap, and an AR-15 semi-automatic rifle on the backseat of his car. He could have you abducted, murdered, and disposed of by a professional contract killer. He could plant a car bomb where your vehicle explodes upon ignition. Or, he could be more direct, attack you, beat you into critical condition, ram the Glock down your throat, squeeze the trigger, and clear your mind. Permanently.

There's an indeterminable percentage of men who will execute the women who cheated on them, the clandestine lovers they cheated with, and then end their own lives in murder-suicides. There's an indeterminable percentage of women who will do the same, so remember that if you're cheating on your fiancée, girlfriend, or wife.

I know how hard it is to turn sex down. It can be next to impossible if you have a horny, beautiful woman ready to take your dick in every hole and fulfill all of your sexual fantasies, but it's not worth placing your life at risk for another man's fiancee, girlfriend, or wife. Your life and good health are precious, you want to protect them for as long as possible, and a good way to do that is to avoid having sex with women who are in relationships with other men. Does this make sense? It certainly ought to. Avoid dealing with women who have boyfriends, fiancés, and husbands.

25 APR 18 (WED)
1606/The Valley
Mission Hills, Los Angeles, California

CHAPTER 24

End

Hail, faithful reader! You made it to the end of our journey and finished your first full run through *How To Hook Up With And Date Beautiful Women*. Was this your first time reading this book?

Yes? Great! Read it again.

No? Great! Read it again.

It takes time for new information to sink in and take hold. This is your user's guide to the game of getting women for casual sex. Refer back to it as often as needed.

Do you still think it's difficult to hook up with beautiful women? It's as difficult as you choose to make it. When you see a comely woman who makes your dick hard, all that stands between you and her are air, opportunity, and your fear of rejection. Read this guide until you understand that. Read this guide until approaching comely women for casual sex becomes second nature to you.

Do you still think it's difficult to take beautiful women out on dates? It's as difficult as you choose to make it. When you see a comely woman you want to date, all that stands between you and her are air, opportunity, your lack of confidence, and low self-esteem. Read this guide until you understand that. Read this guide until dating the beautiful women you want to fuck becomes second nature to you.

Thank you for buying this book and making it a part of your life.

You made a solid decision you won't regret. Follow me at westcoastwriter.com and join the mailing list.

The Cnif + Naedl Company intends to capture 1% of the North American publishing industry's revenue, and I thank you for your support in helping us to reach that goal. I appreciate you and thank you for your support in my next endeavour. Life is the sweetest madness you will ever know. May it treat you and your loved ones well.

Kind regards,

Dennis Park

25 APR 18 (WED)
1730/The Valley
Casita Del Taco, North Hollywood, Los Angeles, California

About The Author

Dennis Park earned his B.A. in English and Political Science from the University of Michigan. He got fired from his plant job for refusing to kiss ass, and a script he wrote in prison won him a spot in a screenwriting fellowship at the University of Southern California. He drove out to LA and never looked back. Dennis enjoys cannabis, push-ups, Korean fried chicken, and writing about man's inhumanity to man.